Coaching Teachers in

Bilingual and Dual-Language Classrooms

A RESPONSIVE CYCLE FOR
Observation and Feedback

Alexandra Guilamo

Solution Tree | Press

a division of
Solution Tree

555 North Morton Street
Bloomington, IN 47404
800.733.6786 (toll free) / 812.336.7700
FAX: 812.336.7790

email: info@SolutionTree.com
SolutionTree.com

Visit **go.SolutionTree.com/EL** to download the free reproducibles in this book.

Printed in the United States of America

FSC
www.fsc.org
FSC® C012681

The mark of
responsible forestry

Library of Congress Cataloging-in-Publication Data

Names: Guilamo, Alexandra, author.
Title: Coaching teachers in bilingual and dual-language classrooms : a
   responsive cycle for observation and feedback / Alexandra Guilamo.
Description: Bloomington, IN : Solution Tree Press, [2020] | Includes
   bibliographical references and index.
Identifiers: LCCN 2019017615 | ISBN 9781949539233
Subjects: LCSH: Teachers--Training of--United States. | Education,
   Bilingual--United States. | Employees--Coaching of--United States. |
   Observation (Educational method) | Feedback (Psychology)
Classification: LCC LC3728 .G85 2020 | DDC 370.71/1--dc23
LC record available at https://lccn.loc.gov/2019017615

Solution Tree
Jeffrey C. Jones, CEO
Edmund M. Ackerman, President

Solution Tree Press
President and Publisher: Douglas M. Rife
Associate Publisher: Sarah Payne-Mills
Art Director: Rian Anderson
Managing Production Editor: Kendra Slayton
Senior Production Editor: Christine Hood
Content Development Specialist: Amy Rubenstein
Copy Editor: Miranda Addonizio
Proofreader: Elisabeth Abrams
Text and Cover Designer: Laura Cox
Editorial Assistant: Sarah Ludwig

Acknowledgments

A very special thank you to my family for your amazing support and selflessness. I am forever indebted to your willingness to share my love and passion with children and schools in districts across the United States. And to my extended family and friends in those schools who have been such amazing partners in advocacy and learning—you have allowed this work to be realized. Thank you for believing in, encouraging, questioning, and advocating for the very best for your students.

Solution Tree Press would like to thank the following reviewers:

Jennifer Arias
ELL and English Instructor
Adlai Stevenson High School
Lincolnshire, Illinois

Theresa Duran-Fuentes
Bilingual Resource Teacher
Desert View Elementary School
Los Lunas, New Mexico

José Medina
Chief Educational Advocate
Dr. José Medina: Educational Solutions
Washington, DC

Judith Ravina
Director of Dual-language and ENL
   Programs
Mamaroneck Union Free School District
Mamaroneck, New York

Visit **go.SolutionTree.com/EL** to download the
free reproducibles in this book.

Table of Contents

Reproducible pages are in italics.

About the Author

Alexandra Guilamo is a leading expert in the education and effective leadership of bilingual and dual-language educators and language learners. As a language learner herself, Alexandra has spent more than twenty years serving a wide range of language learners. She is a former teacher, academic coach, elementary school principal, and district-level director in highly diverse urban and suburban school districts. This range of experiences has equipped her with a unique lens that brings together a deep knowledge of second language acquisition, the guidance of evidence-based practices, and an ability to tailor supports to the distinct contexts and needs of each school she serves.

She is the founder and current chief equity and achievement officer at TaJu Educational Solutions, a company dedicated to meeting the needs of language learners while ensuring access and social justice for all students. Alexandra's skilled, flexible, and evidence-based approach to supporting a range of educators has resulted in dramatic improvement for programs across the country. Because of this, she has now worked with school, district, regional, and state leaders and teachers in more than forty states across the United States to provide a range of professional development, job-embedded coaching, technical assistance, and program evaluation support.

Alexandra is a member of and frequently presents at the National Association for Bilingual Education (NABE), TESOL International Association, Public Policy Professional Council (PPPC), Association for Supervision and Curriculum Development (ASCD), National Council of State Title III Directors, Illinois Association of Multilingual Multicultural Education (IAMME), Learning Forward, and Illinois Reading Council (IRC).

Alexandra received a bachelor's degree from Drake University, a master's degree from National Louis University, and is completing her doctorate from Concordia University.

To learn more about Alexandra Guilamo's work, visit www.tajulearning.com, or follow her @TajuLearning on Twitter.

To book Alexandra Guilamo for professional development, contact pd@ SolutionTree.com.

Introduction

I have served in many different roles as an educator, but the two roles I loved most were those of academic coach and elementary school principal. They weren't always easy, but they gave me the opportunity to focus on the most important parts of education—teaching and learning. During those years, I refined many of the skills I needed to work with diverse teachers on implementing powerful practices to accelerate the growth of *all* students. After all, making a difference in the lives of students is the reason I went into education.

I loved shutting out the world, going into classrooms to observe a lesson, and working side by side with teachers to zero in on a goal that could improve student learning. This was something I did in every classroom—monolingual, bilingual, dual-language, special education, and so on. The teachers never questioned the ability to move in and out of each of these spaces with such ease. Being bilingual myself and having taught language learners all my life provided a sense of confidence in knowing what to look for and a strong credibility with the teachers with whom I worked.

As a principal and academic coach, I observed instruction in English, Spanish, and Arabic. Since I transitioned into my role as a consultant, I've observed lessons in nearly a thousand classrooms in Spanish, English, Mandarin, Arabic, Somali, Hmong, Polish, German, and many more languages.

When I first began my consulting work, I approached interactions with these new and amazing teachers with one basic assumption: that everyone observed teachers who use a language other than English with the same ease, lens, and process that had become second nature to me. And yet, with each school and district visit, it became more and more clear that this was not the case.

As I work with schools across the United States, I'm still amazed at the overwhelming pressures on the shoulders of bilingual and dual-language teachers. These pressures include keeping up with pacing, implementing buildingwide initiatives that require anywhere from fifteen to sixty minutes of already limited instructional time, and of course, increasing achievement. These pressures are riddled with challenges, such as the absence of a viable curriculum (Marzano, 2003), valid and reliable data, time to teach the required standards, and basic supports that are staples for monolingual teachers.

As a former administrator, I believe that bilingual and dual-language teachers should and must be accountable for producing results. Students come to school counting on receiving an education that will prepare them for the future. But due to the unique challenges they face, the message that bilingual and dual-language teachers receive is to produce more with less. There seems to be an unspoken expectation that these teachers can produce the same academic results as their monolingual colleagues while having to teach an additional set of standards, translate huge amounts of print resources, and constantly justify why their classrooms have to look different—as if the program itself was the way to achievement.

Confronting and overcoming these challenges can be mentally and physically exhausting, resulting in immense turnover and creating a teacher shortage that could have huge consequences for U.S. students, schools, and the future workforce necessary for any society to thrive.

As educators, we must not force bilingual and dual-language teachers to simply make it work under these conditions. At a minimum, we must share the responsibility of providing all teachers with equal access to the same supports for improving their effectiveness. While aspects of the process are more challenging than others, leaving these teachers to fend for themselves is no longer tolerable or sustainable.

As schools determine how to ensure the academic success and language development of every language learner now mandated by the Every Student Succeeds Act (ESSA), supporting teacher effectiveness must be the focus of discussion and action. This work of observing, providing feedback, and coaching teachers is critical. But this can't be just any support, especially if it conflicts with the research or focuses on using materials and initiatives rather than student thinking and increasingly complex language development.

The challenges teachers face in getting quality feedback and support always seem to reflect a few reoccurring themes.

- Support personnel in the building did not observe the teachers because they didn't know how it was possible to observe without speaking the language.
- District personnel only observed and evaluated teachers for the required two to four observations per year because no building coach or evaluator spoke the program language.

- District personnel observed teachers using a business-as-usual approach and offered feedback that was counterproductive to the very principles that were most essential to the program model in which they taught.
- Teachers felt disconnected and abandoned while still hungry for collaboration and opportunities to grow.

I realized that it wasn't only bilingual and dual-language teachers who needed support to grow their practice. Rather, school and district personnel who are there to coach and support the teachers who navigate this gray area of learning content and language were also at a loss. How would teachers get the coaching they needed if the coaches didn't, couldn't, or struggled to enter into classrooms to provide meaningful and constructive help? Interestingly, it wasn't only English-speaking coaches who steered clear of these classrooms. Even coaches who spoke the language of instruction struggled to understand teacher practice and how to improve student learning.

To answer the preceding question, I must first acknowledge that coaches who support bilingual and dual-language teachers face unique circumstances and challenges, and therefore need a different model for coaching and observation—one that helps them overcome the issues created by language barriers and misconceptions about the coaching process. This book presents a responsive observation and feedback cycle that diminishes the challenges of observing in the complex and diverse classrooms that serve language learners and helps coaches who support bilingual and dual-language teachers acquire the skills and perspectives necessary to effectively coach in these classrooms. In doing so, coaches will be better prepared to actively develop and engage in a fair and meaningful process that can transform current and future options for students.

The Time Is Now

You might ask, "Why now?" Why have the number of bilingual and dual-language classrooms increased so much that they have reached a breaking point that demands a new model of coaching? The reality is that classrooms have undergone massive demographic changes. In fact, 2014 marked the first time in U.S. history that students who were once considered the minority are now the majority (Maxwell, 2014). Maxwell (2014) states: "This fall, for the first time, the number of Latino, African-American, and Asian students in public K–12 classrooms is expected to surpass the number of non-Hispanic whites." In particular, educators have struggled with how to sufficiently and effectively serve the number of English learners (ELs) in K–12 schools.

English learners are a very diverse group, and we know that different states use a range of terms to discuss that diversity. However, for the purpose of this text, I will use the term *bilingual and dual-language students*. I have chosen to use this term because it refers to students who are developing two language and literacy systems as part of their K–12 bilingual and dual-language educational experiences. These are students who emerge as truly bilingual and biliterate, rather than simply proficient in the English language.

To some, the distinction between biliterate and proficient is a small one. However, it is an important distinction in terminology that plays a role in teacher choices for leveraging educational theory and implementing best practices.

Before 2010, bilingual and dual-language students were present in only a handful of states. The Migration Policy Institute reports that between 2011 and 2015, the percentage of K–3 emergent bilinguals was 44.6 percent in California, 42.6 percent in New York, 45.3 percent in Texas, and 44.7 percent in Florida, while other states like West Virginia, South Dakota, and Kansas hovered between 1 percent and 5 percent (Park, O'Toole, & Katsiaficas, 2017).

But this trend of bilingual and dual-language students residing in only a handful of states has dramatically changed. In fact, between 2000 and 2017, "the young Dual Language Learner (DLL) population in the United States has grown by 24 percent" (Park et al., 2017, p. 1). What does that mean for schools across the United States? Based on 2017 figures, more than one-third of all U.S. students in grades preK through third grade are emergent bilinguals (Park et al., 2017). This immense growth in the number of bilingual and dual-language students has brought about a new education imperative for us all: improve the quality and impact of instruction for this growing number of students or face the consequences of a majority of the U.S. population without the expertise and training necessary to be our future workforce.

As schools rethink how to ensure high-quality instruction for bilingual and dual-language learners, sweeping school-level, program-level, and policy changes are happening across the United States. One of the policy changes that influenced other U.S. states was California's repeal of English-only requirements with Proposition 58 in 2016 (Hopkinson, 2017). This move has opened the door to a growing number of options for schools to leverage bilingual and dual-language programs— programs that have proven to be more effective than English-only models that result in a consistent pattern of failure for language learners (Collier & Thomas, 2004).

Educators must take steps to ensure that the growing number of bilingual and dual-language students served by an expanding number of programs and schools is set up for success. The teachers in these schools are in varying stages of expertise and ownership and need support. With the range of teachers, students, programs, and situations, the best form of support is a coach who is successfully and consistently able to help teachers effectively drive student achievement.

Consequences of Failing to Act

If we don't develop and maintain supports for language learners, their teachers, and their coaches, the consequences will be serious. In failing to act, we turn our backs on the fundamental belief of education to place student learning at the center of teaching. In acting to prevent failure, schools must ensure that all teachers have access to building-level supports designed to improve student learning, especially for classrooms that serve the complex needs of language learners. With the rapidly growing number of bilingual and dual-language students represented in our schools, our collective future depends on their success.

There are many program models that serve these students. However, the observation and feedback cycle offered in this book works just as effectively in each model. The observation and feedback cycle offered in this book supports each of the four most widely used models: (1) dual-language (DL) programs, (2) transitional bilingual education (TBE), (3) foreign language immersion (FLI) programs, and (4) transitional programs of instruction (TPI), such as English as a second language (ESL) and English to speakers of other languages (ESOL). Teachers using these programs truly need the type of coaching and collaboration outlined in this book. Table I.1 (page 6) provides a brief description of these four models, or program types.

Each of the four program models contains distinctive characteristics. Additionally, one of four different formats can be used for each of the four distinctive models. These formats include one-way programs, two-way programs, early-exit programs, and late-exit programs (see figure I.1).

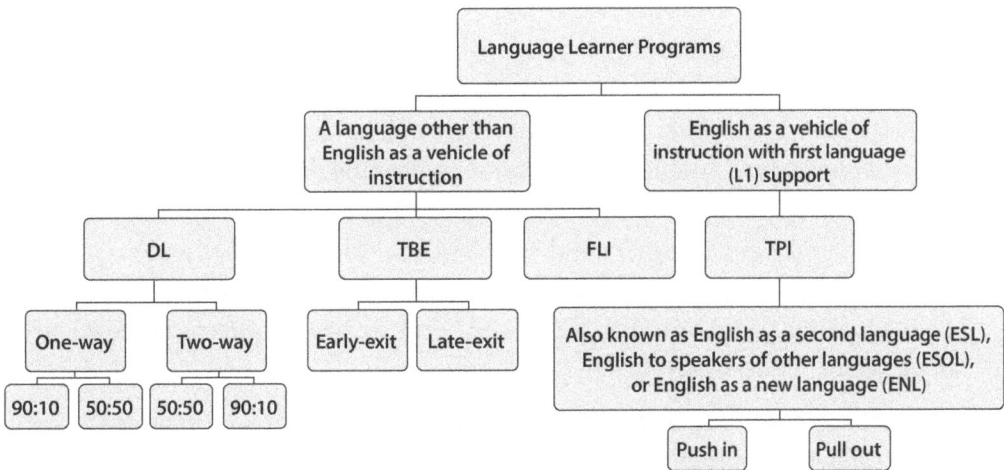

Figure I.1: Program models and classrooms organized under the language learner programs umbrella.

Table I.1: Program Models and Descriptions

Program Model	Acronym	Description
Dual-Language Programs	DL	In this program, students receive 50 percent of their school day (instructional and noninstructional time) in English and 50 percent in the target language (language other than English).
Transitional Bilingual Education	TBE	In this program, classrooms generally begin in kindergarten with 90 percent of instruction in the target language and 10 percent of instruction in English. With each grade after kindergarten, students further increase their percentage of English instruction until they transition to English only.
Foreign Language Immersion Programs	FLI	In this program, non–language learners receive instruction in the target language for a specified number of courses (for example, French social studies or Spanish science) as enrichment.
Transitional Programs of Instruction	TPI (such as English as a second language [ESL] and English to speakers of other languages [ESOL])	In these programs, language specialists either push into the general education classroom or pull students out of the classroom to teach language learners from a variety of language backgrounds; they often leverage native language during instruction for language learners early in their English acquisition.

One-way programs serve students who represent one linguistic group and subsequently one direction of language learning—for example, all Spanish-speaking students who are all learning English. Two-way programs serve students in two linguistic groups and therefore two directions of language learning, such as in the case of a classroom containing half Chinese-speaking and half English-speaking students who must learn from each other. Early-exit programs focus on early education, and typically students leave them between second and third grade. Late-exit programs allow a longer period for second language acquisition, often spanning seven academic years, and provide content-area instruction in the student's first language in the earlier years of the program.

These program models and accompanying structures hope to change the pattern of failure for bilingual and dual-language students. Yet, in order to reap the benefits of a program model, teachers must have the essential knowledge, skills, and attitudes necessary for developing and implementing an effective educational experience that balances all the needs of students and the program.

While some program models may explicitly include the goals of bilingualism and biliteracy, grade-level academic achievement across two languages, and sociocultural competence, other models of bilingual education focus simply on students' English literacy and overall grade-level academic achievement. And while more options create greater possibilities for a better future, they also require schools to develop their staff expertise. Few teacher preparation programs truly build the expertise that is essential to teacher success with bilingual and dual-language students.

According to the National Comprehensive Center for Teacher Quality in 2009–2010, twenty-five states and the District of Columbia have certification requirements for a teaching certificate in bilingual education (López, 2014). However, many teachers are still not prepared for the realities of meeting the diverse needs they encounter. This means that even if teachers are fluent in all languages that their students know, they may lack an understanding of the pedagogy, authentic literacy development, instructional planning, and other expertise they need to be successful bilingual and dual-language educators.

In truth, even as program model design and effectiveness remain of critical importance, one of the greatest barriers to student success is the lack of qualified teachers for bilingual and dual-language programs. In the 2017–2018 school year, thirty-two states reported teacher shortages of bilingual and dual-language teachers (Liebtag & Haugen, 2015). Shortages stem from a number of challenging issues. One such issue is that schools ask these teachers to engage in long hours of translating materials, and they often need to modify curricular resources that were not designed for bilingual and dual-language students after having been told they simply have to make it work.

The extra responsibilities of bilingual and dual-language teachers can make the job very challenging. This challenge is only exacerbated by the fact that these teachers often work in relative isolation. They must find ways to effectively design instruction without collaborative planning with their peers and meet school standards of success with little or no support. Bilingual and dual-language teachers are in particular danger of burning out early, and talented, caring teachers may avoid the career path due to the expected heavy workload in absence of the emotional support of other educators.

Simple coaching support (from other teachers, school-based instructional leaders, and district-level supports) could not only provide bilingual and dual-language teachers with strategies, time, and materials to teach more effectively but also with collegial respect for their work that reduces low morale (Harris & Sandoval-Gonzalez, 2017).

In an attempt to address the current and impending teacher shortages, many states have tried to offer other means of staffing these programs. Strategies to encourage bilingual and dual-language teaching careers include "creating alternative certification pathways, establishing partnerships with other countries to identify teachers with appropriate partner language skills, [and] increasing recruitment efforts" (López, 2014). These strategies have helped get bilingual and dual-language instructors into schools. However, because they lack the preservice education provided through more traditional certification paths, they need intensive support through classroom observation and coaching to help them be effective in the classroom.

These teachers—often the youngest and least experienced ones to enter the field—need guidance and support to continually build their capacity. As new teachers, they actively want to be part of an education community that learns and grows together in meaningful ways. In order to provide that, education leaders must be well-versed in the benefits and advantages of quality programs. They must also accept and be prepared to leverage the opportunity to observe and coach teachers who arguably need support the most, regardless of whether they speak the language of instruction (Harris & Sandoval-Gonzalez, 2017).

The Definition of a Coach

In this book, I use the term *coach* broadly to identify people who might wear a number of hats, which is often the case in education. Most important, a coach is not defined by a title. A coach can be a principal, an instructional or a dual-language specialist, a grade-level leader, or a coordinator. More than an official job title, it is what educators practice—how they leverage knowledge, skills, modes of communication, and so on—during their interactions with each teacher that helps us understand who the coach should be. This book gives coaches and prospective coaches the information and tools they need to enter classrooms and improve teacher practice, which in turn leads to higher student achievement.

By providing critical tools for coaching, this book develops coaches' ability to build relationships defined by open communication, so the coach and teacher can work to improve the most high-leverage skills, strategies, and practices. It provides coaches with a process they can use to help improve the confidence of the teachers they work with, helping them use objective evidence they receive from observation to more accurately determine their own strengths and opportunities to improve their practice. Finally, guiding questions and tools will help coaches build confidence in their own abilities to fairly and consistently consider what is unique and different about bilingual and dual-language classrooms and work with teachers to implement effective strategies.

In This Book

I used a number of contexts as guides in developing this book. The work I have done with hundreds of coaches, building administrators, district leaders, and educators in a range of program models helped me shape the challenges and needed supports into a schema. In addition, I referenced theoretical frameworks from dual-language education, bilingual education, various evaluation instruments, various coaching models, and several change models in developing the observation and feedback cycle and the action-planning templates embedded in every chapter.

Part 1 includes chapters 1–3 and answers the question, What essential skills or perspectives do coaches need to focus the observation and feedback cycle into continuous opportunities to transform bilingual and dual-language instruction? Chapter 1 introduces the goals, challenges, and keys for creating a fair observation and feedback cycle when observing instruction that leverages another language. It also provides an overview of the unique stages and steps included in the observation and feedback cycle. Chapter 2 explores the eight goals of the observation and feedback cycle and theoretical frameworks coaches need to identify effective practices within the context of the program and school mission and vision. Finally, chapter 3 helps coaches distinguish what effective feedback looks, sounds, and feels like when it leads to action and improved student outcomes.

Part 2 includes chapters 4–7 and answers the question, What are the four stages of the observation and feedback cycle, and how can teachers consistently and correctly engage in this cycle if they don't speak the language of instruction? Chapter 4 describes the changes in mindset teachers and coaches must establish to lay the foundation for the observation and feedback cycle. Chapter 5 describes the actions that both teacher and coach need to take prior to the observation to minimize the impact of language on the quality of evidence the observer is able to collect. Chapter 6 explains the observation process for coaches. This process is the heart of the book because it encompasses the most important and difficult work that a coach must do. Bilingual and dual-language classrooms are dynamic environments. They require the coach to think creatively, recognize creativity, and be able to trust his or her own judgment, yet remain open to new ideas and other perspectives. In order to generate value from this process, coaches must be able to articulate what they observe and share their insights about complex behaviors and interactions. Chapter 7 describes the post-observation conference, offering a clear model for coaches that connects the act of gathering accurate evidence from a variety of sources with identifying high-leverage feedback.

The book concludes with two appendices, which take a more detailed look at various program models and offer answers to the most frequently asked questions by coaches and teachers.

When coaches understand the complexities of these classrooms and have the tools to overcome the language barrier, they realize how much they can contribute to teacher and student success. Bilingual and dual-language teachers serve the fastest-growing student demographic in the United States, and they deserve and require these supports. That is the goal of this book—to provide the tools that coaches need to level the playing field in schools. In the end, structuring schools to provide equal access to instructional supports is the only way to make it work for all teachers and transform outcomes for students.

Part 1

Essential Skills for Implementing the Observation and Feedback Cycle

CHAPTER 1

Fair Observations in Bilingual and Dual-Language Classrooms

Many coaches have asked me about the need for a new set of tools that ensures a fair observation and feedback cycle for bilingual and dual-language classrooms. They want to trust the efficacy of the tools at their immediate disposal. Their questions usually sound something like this: "Aren't the district-adopted observation and evaluation frameworks designed for just that? Don't they ensure quality of instruction that leads to student achievement? If so, how could using anything else be considered fairer?" When it comes to language learners, the answer is both *yes* and *no*. It is not a question of what these frameworks were designed to do. Teacher evaluation frameworks are used by every school to evaluate the quality and effectiveness of teachers against a common definition of good teaching. These frameworks are used by building administrators and coaches not only for evaluating teacher quality, but to guide coaches in the capacity-building efforts with teachers, as well.

Instead, it is more a question of how to get the right evidence during an observation. The important point to understand is that if we are to have fair observations in bilingual and dual-language classrooms, we must have clear practices in place for observing effectively and accurately, regardless of the school- or districtwide adopted teacher evaluation framework.

However, after reviewing the statewide evaluation frameworks and teacher evaluation rubrics adopted by districts across the United States, it became abundantly clear that these frameworks lack clarity in how to gather data when observing, especially when the observation is in another language, despite the vast number of programs that exist (Danielson, 2011, 2013; Marshall, 2013; Marzano, 2001b).

The failure to acknowledge the uniqueness of bilingual and dual-language classrooms creates huge challenges for the observing coach and the teachers they observe alike (Higher Educators in Linguistically Diverse Education, 2015). Without processes for the accurate identification of best practice in bilingual and dual-language settings and for collection of evidence from lessons delivered in a language that the coach does not speak, observations will struggle to be fair and effective at improving student outcomes. Let's begin by defining what fair means in the observation and feedback cycle.

A Definition of *Fair*

In order to establish best practices, we need to establish a shared definition of *fair observation* and what it means for our practice. *Fair* means honest and bias-free. Fair means embracing actions and systems that ensure justice for everyone affected. Most important, to be fair requires a legitimate approach with clearly defined rules or conditions. Observations must credibly put student learning across language, culture, and content at the center of the process.

This may or may not be the definition many think of for *fair*, but any definition that fails to reach the level of social justice, equity, and access is simply not good enough. So, what does this mean for the process of observing in the language learning classroom? It means that we need more useful tools to minimize biases that stem from what we expect to see in monolingual classrooms. Unfortunately, most of the current observation and evaluation frameworks don't contain these tools, which make them only fairish.

The Challenges of Current Teacher Evaluation Frameworks

Many teacher observation and evaluation frameworks are valuable tools in defining the ingredients of effective teaching, but they do not recognize the strengths and challenges of English learners (ELs) (Fenner, Kozik, & Cooper, 2014). None require teachers to have high levels of proficiency in a language other than English. None require teachers to demonstrate how they use their knowledge or skills to analyze academic language proficiency so they can differentiate and adapt their instruction to ensure that their students access grade-level learning. In fact, none identify the evidence-based practices that embody the most effective bilingual and dual-language classrooms.

More concerning is the number of assumptions about highly effective content, curriculum, and tools that are apparent in most of the observation protocols—assumptions that often conflict with language learner needs. Assumptions may include but are not limited to the following.

- Word walls that are organized by the alphabet are beneficial.
- Unit tests accurately assess content learning rather than language proficiency even for emergent bilinguals.
- Only one language will be used by students at all times during the lesson.

Take, for example, one assumption that frustrates primary teachers who leverage Spanish literacy as part of their programs. No framework defines what early Spanish literacy content, instruction, outcomes, and resources highly effective teachers should use to develop early literacy, but many educators assume the best resources to use are those based on research that supports systematic, synthetic phonics instruction (Slavin, Lake, Chambers, Cheung, & Davis, 2009). Naturally, these teachers expect to see content that includes phonics, effective phonics methods, assessments that measure students' progress with phonics skills, and lots of phonics-based resources that they should use with fidelity.

The problem isn't the strategic alignment that reflects highly effective teaching and learning. The problem is the assumption that phonics is necessary for all students. Systematic, synthetic phonics instruction is not necessary for early Spanish literacy. The sequence of letter sounds and emphasis of building on those sounds to create English words tend to confuse students and delay the most effective research-based methods for Spanish literacy. So, what happens to teachers who could accelerate early literacy in Spanish but are mandated to use English phonics, English phonics–based assessments, and phonics-based resources with fidelity? It's like trying to be a vegetarian while eating pork; it's counterproductive. It's a struggle that usually ends with stressed teachers due to the pressure following the assumed definition of highly effective practice, and it ends with students not having their needs met.

Even coaches who do not carry these common assumptions, or who are able to see possibilities beyond them, are likely to make many faulty inferences during observations in bilingual and dual-language classrooms. Why are these faulty inferences so likely? When coaches are unable to recognize the unique ingredients of quality bilingual and dual-language instruction and the complex needs of bilingual and dual-language students, there's a high probability that coaches will jump to conclusions about parts of the observation and add meanings to lessons that do not exist, ending with inaccurate understandings of the teaching and learning that occurred. These are hardly conditions for fairness.

A fair observation process should help observers look for the right ingredients across a range of program models:

> The literature suggests the importance of the following variables: (a) which language of instruction is used, and for what content (Heras, 1994); (b) how the first and second languages may be used together (Heras, 1994); (c) how students are physically grouped for instruction (Strong, 1986), (d) what types of learning activities occur, and with what opportunity for student language use (Berducci, 1993), and (e) how listening, speaking, writing and reading communication modes are utilized for language learning (Krashen & Biber, 1988). (Bruce, et al., 1997, p. 24)

Even though these variables address essential ingredients in bilingual and dual-language classrooms, they are absent from traditional teacher evaluation frameworks. Teacher evaluation frameworks are even less helpful when coaches don't fully understand the language of instruction (a reality for the majority of coaches in bilingual and dual-language programs). In these cases, the probability of coaches making inferences that lead to inaccurate judgments is even higher. The probability increases because listening to the words that teachers say, questions they ask and print and post around the room, and other instances of language use, is ingrained in what most coaches do every day. Even for the most experienced coaches, it is almost impossible to have an honest and fair observation and feedback cycle with so much room for error.

The preceding issues represent significant barriers to creating a fair system. Observation frameworks are supposed to improve student learning through clear, defined expectations and practices. Yet this formula rarely accounts for any of the ingredients that are defined as most effective for bilingual and dual-language students. According to Jennifer F. Samson and Brian A. Collins (2012), "It seems reasonable that when teachers receive clearly articulated, consistent expectations on how best to work with ELLs as part of their preparation, certification, and evaluation, the outcomes for their ELL students will reflect this increased emphasis" (p. 20).

That means that for these frameworks to work, coaches need a more explicit, defined, and legitimate process for how to support teachers' capacity to best work with students, regardless of whether they fully know the language of instruction. It is a shift that is necessary for coaches to honestly and consistently identify and support expectations and variables that improve student learning. Only then can coaches help bilingual and dual-language teachers navigate their individual "competencies or confusions," "strengths or weaknesses," "strategies missed or used," and "evidence of what . . . [students] . . . understand," in service of student success (Andrade, Basurto, Clay, Ruiz, & Escamilla, 1996, p. 7). And when coaches are able to navigate the strengths and challenges of classroom teachers and match bilingual and dual-language teachers with the professional development necessary for success, we see amazing growth for students (Fenner et al., 2014).

The observation and feedback cycle and tools presented in this book provide clear guidance to coaches for how to fairly observe a lesson, especially when they don't understand the language. I do not aim to replace adopted teacher evaluation frameworks. Instead, I present an observation and feedback cycle that is a fair and just means of using such frameworks to improve student learning. When schools use this observation and feedback cycle in concert with teacher evaluation frameworks, they provide a level of neutrality, consistency, and accuracy that supports effective teachers of ELs (Fenner et al., 2014).

The Role of Advocacy in Coaching

One of the most basic mindsets that coaches can transfer from their prior experience is the idea that they must work to improve teacher practice while also advocating to overcome challenges that may stand in the way of teacher effectiveness. Many challenges stand in the way of bilingual and dual-language teachers' ability to be most effective. These challenges include:

- Being used as interpreters and translators rather than having time to plan high-quality instruction
- Receiving no curriculum materials in the language of instruction
- Teaching double the standards and learning targets while being expected to maintain the same pace as monolingual teachers
- Receiving no training in the pedagogy, practices, and strategies that meet the needs of language learners
- Having no process to distinguish struggling or honors-level language learners from the language-learning process
- Being required to use English-only data to determine student progress, needs, and teacher evaluation

Sadly, I could add many more items to this list. This status quo would seem appalling if we were discussing an international baccalaureate (IB) program or gifted classroom. Yet schools still expect EL, DL, and TBE teachers to reach the same level of growth and success with their students despite having fewer opportunities, fewer resources, and fewer tools for success. That's why coaches must be powerful advocates and allies in helping to overcome these challenges and barriers.

This is where coaches from outside the EL, DL, and TBE program have the advantage. It's easier to identify inequities when there's a more equitable reference point. These coaches know the many systems, infrastructures, and supports their schools have to ensure access, equity, and dignity in other programs. Structures like professional development plans, cohesive and viable curricula, collaborative planning, feedback, and use of valid data to drive decision-making processes exist to strengthen the ability to achieve success. Coaches must take action to ensure that the lack of these tools doesn't undermine this success for bilingual and dual-language teachers and students they work with. As coaches provide feedback to teachers, it is critical that they use their monolingual reference point as a sort of check and balance. They might ask themselves, "What would we do if this were happening outside of this program?"

For example, during post-observation conversations, coaches might find themselves discussing with teachers the lack of scaffolds to improve student engagement and learning. In digging deeper into the issue, a coach learns that the teacher didn't have time to create those scaffolds because she spends about eight hours every week translating the curriculum she received into the language other than English (LOTE), even though she has been told that she must teach that content in English. The coach must address this challenge because students learning another language need scaffolds to access the curriculum. Fair and effective coaches will pause to check their monolingual reference point. Would we ask monolingual teachers to spend eight hours translating their districtwide curriculum? Clearly we would not. Therefore, teachers need coaches who see these issues as matters beyond a teacher's control and who will work on teachers' behalf to get rid of those obstacles (Kotter, 2012).

Data Gathering

In the 1980s, schools used open-ended visits and checklists as their methods for gathering observation data. These tools had various components from state to state and provided very little guidance for what to do during observation to objectively determine whether components were strengths or weaknesses. But with time, these tools changed. From the late 1990s to early 2000s, a number of approaches to gathering data during observations posed additional problems for teachers serving language learners (Danielson, 2000; Marzano, 2013). Schools began exchanging checklists for rubrics and providing more parameters around what to do during observations—instructional rounds, classroom walkthroughs, lesson scripting, and so on. Teachers needed these parameters. Some proved to be more conducive to language learning contexts, like the walkthrough protocols that allowed observers to make more open-ended observations around specific focus areas (for example, environment, classroom management, and even engagement and discussion).

Others, however, proved to be detrimental to most bilingual and dual-language contexts. I still hear from bilingual and dual-language educators across the United States about observation "horror stories." In one of the buildings I supported, a teacher begged me to talk with her principal about the following situation: The principal had asked her to teach the lesson in English even though that wasn't reflective of the program and her students were not used to learning content in English. Not only did she have to spend long hours translating the lesson and resources into English, but the students kept responding to her in Spanish. The worst part of the observation for the teacher was when the principal chose one of her new students to talk to, not realizing that the student didn't speak any English. This concluded with the principal reprimanding the teacher before leaving the room for not teaching her class any English, and a teary-eyed new student asking the teacher if it was her fault that her teacher got in trouble.

These sad realities are the result of a data-gathering process that refuses to acknowledge the two observational elephants in the room: (1) the lesson is in a language the observer doesn't speak, and (2) the effectiveness of the lesson has just as much to do with how students improve their language development as with how they master the content. Data-gathering processes must be honest and objective for all classrooms. Many states have tried to accomplish objectivity by standardizing data-gathering protocols, such as the following, that champion limited and controlled practices during all observations.

- Scripting (or recording copious notes that aim to transcribe) what the teacher is saying and doing
- Scripting what the student is saying and doing
- Anchoring data with qualitative markers (for example, time during the lesson, number of students, quantity of instances, and so on)
- Noting and duplicating aspects of the environment (for example, anchor charts, classroom appearance, objectives, and directions on the board)

The designers of these protocols aimed for observational objectivity, unbiased data gathering, and models for what to do next. They meant to establish a judgment-free process for improving teacher quality. But by prioritizing the scripting of language interactions and language use (especially that of the teacher) as the only objective way to collect evidence, they ended any possibility of objectivity for bilingual and dual-language classrooms. And without the written account that scripting offers, qualitative markers lack enough substance to effectively coach.

Without full proficiency in the language, it is difficult for observers to log what the teacher says, what the students say, or any of the word-for-word print environment. Any attempt to do so would be unfair. Coaches and educational advocates must have the sense and courage to refuse a teacher evaluation process that leaves coaches without a clearly defined approach for how to document teaching and learning without understanding the words, visible print, and cultural nuances of bilingual and dual-language classrooms. Both the implementation of specific protocols and the use of common sense to recognize when a protocol will not be effective are attempts to engage in a process with bilingual and dual-language teachers that is highly objective, collaborative, and constructive, but the process cannot be so in the existing context.

What to Expect From the Observation and Feedback Cycle

The observation and feedback cycle is a four-stage process consisting of: (1) an essential mindset shift that frames the foundation for a fair, honest, and collaborative process; (2) the pre-observation conference; (3) the observation; and (4) the post-observation conference.

Essential Mindset Shift That Frames the Foundation

A mindset shift is essential for those who seek to be effective in coaching dual-language and bilingual teachers. This shift includes seven elements: (1) establish trust and confidence; (2) avoid hidden agendas; (3) lead by learning; (4) become an insider, not an outsider; (5) know the right things; (6) ensure confidentiality; and (7) know when to use spotlights and supports. These elements help coaches get in the right frame of mind to lay the foundation for the observation and feedback cycle.

The Pre-Observation Conference

The pre-observation conference allows coaches to closely analyze how the teacher has designed learning to meet the many goals unique to their classroom. The guiding questions provided for coaches offer a set of considerations that must be included in this pre-observation conference for any feedback offered at this stage of the process to be effective.

The Observation

In stage 3 of the observation and feedback cycle, coaches observe instructional delivery using six tasks of notice (see chapter 6, page 77). These tasks of notice are supported by four essential questions (see chapter 6, page 72) that help coaches know how to prioritize their observational notes and identify the area of feedback most likely to accelerate the learning curve for teachers and, by extension, students' learning outcomes. We call these areas of feedback high leverage because they can accelerate the growth process for everyone served.

The Post-Observation Conference

Next, sharing observational notes with bilingual and dual-language teachers gives teachers the opportunity to both self-reflect on what the coach noticed during the observation and answer any clarifying questions that the coach may have regarding something the teacher or students said or wrote that the coach could not fully understand. This time to self-reflect and contextualize language use prepares the coach and teacher to come back together during the final stage of the observation and feedback cycle—the post-observation conference. During the post-observation conference, both educators compare their analysis of the lesson and how effective it was for students. The crucial outcome of this post-observation conference is to accurately identify the decisions made during the observation that were effective as well as moments during the lesson that could have led to greater success had the teacher made a different decision.

This conversation should operate as though the teacher is driving a car with no precise directions for his or her destination. The coach is there to help that teacher think through whether turning left at an intersection is the best route to take or if turning right at the intersection would have helped him or her arrive at the destination more efficiently.

In bilingual and dual-language classrooms, there are multitudes of teaching inter-sections that teachers face every day. We call these intersections *turning points*. Just like the person in the car who could turn left or right, potential turning points in a lesson can range from incorporating scaffolds that match the language proficiency to not addressing smaller misbehaviors that escalated into an argument between students. Analyzing these turning points and looking for patterns in student learning create a trustworthy and reliable framework coaches can use to plan steps for teacher improvement, including a system of actions and supports to ensure their success.

Conclusion

This chapter discussed the challenges in defining a fair observation and feedback cycle. Coaches must strive to provide every teacher with a cycle that is honest and focused on closing the achievement gap of one of our most undereducated student groups. This requires a legitimate process for systematic observation that minimizes the amount of guesswork coaches will do as they use what they've observed throughout the cycle. Coaches don't have to approach observation with a script or nothing approach. They must implement a process that is fair, systematic, and critical in establishing ways to minimize error and maximize the effectiveness of feedback (Pianta & Hamre, 2009). Once that process is in place, they can concentrate on how to give effective feedback. The next chapter discusses the eight goals of the observation and feedback cycle.

The Eight Goals of the Observation and Feedback Cycle

Before outlining the full process of observation and feedback for bilingual and dual-language classrooms, it's important to establish a common definition of the goals of an effective observation and feedback cycle. The goals fall into two categories: (1) goals that work to increase coaching effectiveness and its impact on student success, and (2) goals that work to build teachers' capacity and competence to embrace and implement best practice for bilingual and dual-language learning.

A great deal of research has been devoted to coaching teachers. It is a topic of interest for experts from the broader educational world (Aguilar, 2013; Eisenberg, Eisenberg, Medrich, & Charner, 2017; Fox, Campbell, & Hargrove, 2011; Knight, 2007). While some of these experts' research most adequately addresses coaching practices that exist in every kind of classroom, many such studies exclude the additional, unique needs of bilingual and dual-language classrooms, teachers, and students.

Instructional coaching researcher Jim Knight (2014) advocates for instructional coaching because "most people don't know what it looks like when they do what they do" (p. 138). When I see recordings of presentations and professional development workshops I've delivered, I still feel shocked to hear my own voice. Much in the same vein, bilingual and dual-language teachers rarely have the opportunity to see their teaching and what student learning look like as they conduct the complex combination of steps that take place at any given moment in their classrooms.

This is why bilingual and dual-language teachers need an outside perspective or point of view. They need someone else willing and able to look at their instruction and decision making because they are so involved in teaching that they can't see everything happening or perceive how students are responding (DeWitt, 2014).

Coaches are better able to see those blind spots, or those areas teachers can't see, because they are too close to know what they look like in the moment. Much like in sports, coaches who serve bilingual and dual-language classrooms can help teachers reflect on the decisions they make in the moment, provide feedback about the effectiveness of those decisions, and practice ways to incorporate and develop automaticity around new learning.

Author and speaker Peter DeWitt (2014) suggests that coaching focus on the following four fundamental goals: (1) ensure each encounter helps teachers improve, (2) connect colleagues' successes, (3) provide an outside perspective, and (4) use multiple observations to obtain concrete data on student progress. My experience serving bilingual and dual-language teachers prompts me to add four additional goals: (5) achieve equity, (6) incorporate culture, (7) gather accurate evidence during the observation, and (8) embrace best practices.

The following sections discuss each of these eight goals of effective coaching in bilingual and dual-language classrooms in detail.

Goal 1: Ensure Each Encounter Helps Teachers Improve

The core of any observation and feedback cycle should be a laser focus on student learning. Programmatic alignment is important, but the feedback coaches provide must move beyond mere fidelity to a program model, initiative, or new textbook adoption. Rather, each encounter between coaches and the dual-language and bilingual teachers they serve must be guided by the systematic data collection from authentic assessments that provide meaningful insight into student learning across all program goals. A range of assessments is a vital resource that can guide coaches as they offer teachers a road map of supports aimed at improving student outcomes, and ultimately in evaluating teacher improvement. The key is that both teachers and coaches have access to authentic assessments that (1) are differentiated to match students' language proficiencies and cultural background, and (2) use side-by-side rubrics for content and language.

Are Differentiated to Match Students' Language Proficiencies and Cultural Background

To be effective educators, bilingual and dual-language teachers must shift their thinking about assessment from what they might have used it for in regular classrooms to the specifics of using it in multilingual classrooms. To support these teachers, coaches must first help them find focus in both content and language during the assessment process. If teachers are not intentionally planning for content and language growth, then sadly, they are planning for student failure.

A second but related area of support is helping teachers create assessments that are differentiated for language proficiency. Educational methods expert W. James Popham (2010) states that "there is no such thing as a valid test" (p. 19); rather, we define validity by our interpretation of the test results and what those results mean regarding student learning. This is the irony of the bilingual and dual-language classroom. By their very nature, these classrooms contain students at a range of proficiency levels, many of whom may not have developed the language abilities they need to interact with grade-level content. Most unit-based and teacher-created tests, however, rely on language development levels that teachers already know students don't have. These types of one-size-fits-all tests simply tell teachers what they already know: there is something students didn't understand—maybe the content, but most certainly the language of the test itself. Bilingual and dual-language teachers must, therefore, come up with a better means of collecting, interpreting, and using data about the areas in need of improvement in their classrooms.

Coaches must help teachers adapt assessments to match the level of all students' language proficiency, especially those early in their language journeys. This is easier than it sounds. Simple adaptations like shortening the length of sentences, decreasing the complexity of verb tense, and eliminating slang unfamiliar to non-native speakers can have a huge impact on the readability of a question or set of directions. Additional adaptations help reinforce learning and give teachers more tangible evidence of what students are learning. Adaptations can include giving definitions of nonessential and low-frequency words and providing annotated texts, illustrations, realia, and even tasks that rely more heavily on hands-on experiences and integrate rigorous thinking skills like classifying, sorting, and critiquing.

Teachers must move beyond the once-per-year, state-mandated language proficiency assessments and incorporate varied formative assessment tools (Dunne & Villani, 2007). Educators must have access to real-time data to inform instruction for bilingual and dual-language students if they are to meet the demands of the Common Core State Standards and other next-generation standards. Formative assessment is a key method for obtaining such data. Teachers can use the data from these assessments to focus on the complex needs of bilingual and dual-language students; assist them in mastering grade-level content, concepts, and skills; and help them develop the academic language required to communicate learning. Doing so is the only way to ensure that all students receive the support they need to be successful.

In designing formative assessments for bilingual and dual-language learners, teachers must ensure that their assessments implement the following objectives.

- Promote student learning and application of content and language goals using tasks that are culturally relevant to students.
- Elicit evidence of learning through a variety of tasks (Shavelson, 2006; Shavelson et al., 2008).
- Change the role of teachers, as they learn what students can do. As students show their teachers the expertise they've developed, teachers better know how to help students apply that learning and what additional supports may be needed (Heritage, 2011).
- Use learning progressions to anchor learning goals and monitor learning progress (Heritage, 2008; McManus, 2008).
- Provide meaningful feedback and adjustments that improve instruction for language learners (Heritage, Walqui, & Linquanti, 2012).
- Enable students to become self-regulated and autonomous learners (Hattie & Timperley, 2007).

Figure 2.1 offers a list of ideas for formative assessments that coaches can use collaboratively with teachers.

Have Used	Plan to Use	Rating	Formative Assessment
			Teacher observation
			Questions and discussions
			Projects and presentations
			Graphic organizers or concept maps
			Peer or self-assessments
			Individual whiteboards or response cards
			Analogy prompts
			Quizzes with linguistic modifications
			Think-pair-share, four corners, or other interactive activities
			Exit tickets
			Learning or response logs
			Visual representations
			True-false activities
			Checklists
			Cloze passages

Have Used	Plan to Use	Rating	Formative Assessment
			Constructed responses with illustrating and labeling options
			Categorizing or sequencing activities
			Multiple-choice questions with language modifications
			Portfolios
			Journal entries
			Diagnostic interviews

Figure 2.1: Formative assessment ideas.

*Visit **go.SolutionTree.com/EL** for a free reproducible version of this figure.*

Use Side-by-Side Rubrics for Content and Language

Rubrics must account for the combined content, language, literacy, and cultural goals that make up students' daily experiences as language learners. Bear in mind, too, that students have greater motivation to learn when they see the finish line or goal as something they can attain.

Side-by-side content and language rubrics offer equitable assessment for all language learners. Side-by-side rubrics describe the success criteria of two separate but interdependent learning objectives. One side shows the success criteria demonstrating the extent to which students master rigorous grade-level learning. The other side shows the success criteria for the complexity of language students use based on their language proficiency levels. The side-by-side rubrics in figure 2.2 (page 28) demonstrate how language learners might need different side-by-side rubrics at various points in their language learning journey.

Coaches need to help teachers develop these side-by-side rubrics so teachers receive support in how to maintain the rigor of the standards while having reasonable expectations for student language use. Many teachers are clear when discussing content mastery but not as clear when determining what students need to master a goal that makes sense for where they are in their language journey. The use of side-by-side rubrics helps communicate to students that you know they're still growing, but you expect them to practice the level and complexity of language that they do have. Teachers can differentiate rubrics by changing what they expect from students' language production based on their language proficiency levels.

Narrative Writing		Language Use (Level 1)		Narrative Writing		Language Use (Level 5)	
One story or event is well developed.	___ points	High-frequency words	___ points	One story or event is well developed.	___ points	All parts of the narrative are understandable.	___ points
The narrative includes characters or a narrator.	___ points	Pictures with words that describe them	___ points	The narrative includes characters or a narrator.	___ points	New vocabulary and expressions are used in descriptions.	___ points
The sequence of events in the story is clear.	___ points	One full sentence that uses the sentence starter	___ points	The sequence of events in the story is clear.	___ points	There are both simple and compound sentences.	___ points
Dialogue is used.	___ points			Dialogue is used.	___ points	There are three or more paragraphs.	___ points
The story includes at least three well-described details about the characters' thoughts, feelings, and actions.	___ points	Sentence starter is spelled correctly.	___ points	The story includes at least three well-described details about the characters' thoughts, feelings, and actions.	___ points	Correct verbs are used.	___ points
						All paragraphs begin with transitions.	___ points

Figure 2.2: Example side-by-side rubrics.

Visit go.SolutionTree.com/EL for a free reproducible version of this figure.

Goal 2: Connect Colleagues' Successes

The goal of curating and connecting educators' successes may seem odd to some coaches who embrace and welcome their shared responsibility to bilingual and dual-language teachers and the students they serve. However, connecting successes should be a goal for all coaches for a number of reasons. First, all learning requires some level of social interaction. We need to discuss and problem solve areas that aren't quite clear and make sense of learning in light of prior beliefs that may no longer hold true. These social interactions often take much longer than coaches have for any one teacher. Not only that, but connecting successful teachers with colleagues who need support opens the possibility for those teachers to ask for help when they need it the most. Connecting a more successful colleague with one who is struggling has the added benefit of empowering teachers to solve problems without relying on just the observation and feedback cycle as their sole system of support.

Most important, however, connecting successful colleagues with those needing help (both from within one's own school and from other nearby programs) allows coaches who only speak English to have access to a whole new world of support for bilingual and dual-language teachers that they can't provide themselves. By connecting effective bilingual and dual-language teachers from similar program models with successful strategies, tools, and approaches that better meet students' needs, coaches can offer bilingual and dual-language teachers access to a more responsive process for professional development.

Access to greater equity in ongoing and personalized support is vital when coaches don't know the language of instruction or the appropriate strategies for their emergent bilinguals. This responsive coaching, further developed in chapter 7 as part of stage 4 of the observation and feedback cycle (the post-observation conference, page 101), involves five key actions. These actions include: (1) share the data collected during the observation; (2) clarify misconceptions that may exist in the coach's observations; (3) identify trends of success regarding instructional planning, delivery, and assessment; (4) consider multiple cause-and-effect relationships; and (5) verify earliest possible challenges to use as leverage points for the four essential questions.

Goal 3: Provide an Outside Perspective

The observation and feedback cycle gives bilingual and dual-language teachers a chance to see the process of teaching and learning from a different angle than their own. It is a unique point of view that comes from being inside a classroom during the delivery of a lesson and being an outsider from students' focus or any personal attachment to the lesson. For that reason, the outside perspective that coaches offer during the observation and feedback cycle can provide powerful insight for teachers. At times, teachers are convinced that the image in the mirror is distorted and warped like funhouse mirrors at a carnival. For example, a teacher might see lots of students talking and interpret that as a loud, poorly managed classroom rather than recognize it as a meaningful application of social and academic language supporting content and language growth. Will these views constantly force teachers to justify and defend what they are doing and why it is necessary? Other times, teachers will see and embrace the images shown to them. In either case, bilingual and dual-language teachers are more likely to be willing participants in the coaching process when they see that their coach's feedback reflects a deep understanding of best practice for improving student outcomes.

It's often helpful for coaches to seek their own network of support to help them understand their own misconceptions or misinformation about instruction in bilingual and dual-language classrooms. All coaches have aspects of the teaching and learning process that they are better at supporting than others. For some coaches, it is in a content area like mathematics; for others, it is with strategies like those used for student engagement. For coaches who are working with bilingual and dual-language teachers, it may seem like the entire teaching and learning process in these classrooms is its own unfamiliar language. Coaches who want to overcome their own learning curve will need the support of a coaching or support network. Coaches should be comfortable with accepting guidance from colleagues to help them through the process, while never veering from a strong focus on student learning and results.

A coaching support network depends on the district and building and coaches' access to certain resources. The following list can serve as a solid starting point for new coaches seeking constructive feedback and validation for their work with bilingual and dual-language teachers.

- Biliteracy or dual-language specialists
- Bilingual lead teachers or coordinators
- Administrators
- District-level directors or coordinators
- District coaching networks
- English as a second language (ESL) or second language acquisition (SLA) departments
- Assessment and accountability departments
- Title III departments
- State resource center or English learner division
- Research organizations and evidence-based consortiums
  - » Center for Applied Linguistics (CAL)
  - » Center for Advanced Research on Language Acquisition (CARLA)

» TESOL International Association
» American Council on the Teaching of Foreign Languages (ACTFL)
- National affiliations, local organizations, and other conferences
  » National Association for Bilingual Education (NABE)
  » La Cosecha
  » Defense Language Institute (DLI)
- Office of English Language Acquisition (OELA)

Goal 4: Use Multiple Observations to Obtain Concrete Data on Student Progress

Bilingual and dual-language teachers need sound and concrete data on student development in both content and language standards. All too often, the only language assessment students receive is the assessment mandated annually for language learners. These data are not enough to help teachers plan, adjust, and effectively support the range of needs they must meet every day.

One of the best strategies coaches can use to increase their observational accuracy is to observe a range of lessons. Coaches should not rely on only one observation to measure teaching effectiveness. One observation, even in the best of circumstances, represents only a glimpse of the totality of skills, abilities, and effectiveness of any teacher to meet the needs of all learners across content, language, literacy, and cultural goals.

While there is never a right or wrong observation, there are more-or-less accurate interpretations of what happened in a lesson and more-or-less effective recommendations for what can improve student learning. Because of this, coaches should seek ways to improve the accuracy of their interpretations and the effectiveness of their recommendations.

Observing bilingual and dual-language teachers across content areas (for example, mathematics, reading, or social studies) helps coaches confirm observations or interpretations and decrease errors caused by assumptions and personal biases. Through strategic observations of teachers in a range of contexts, languages, times, and days of the week, coaches limit the possibility that any one isolated observation will mislead them (Andrade et al., 1996).

Multiple opportunities to observe teaching and learning using the tasks of notice allow coaches to get a more authentic view of what regularly happens in the classroom. This increase in frequency and range lessens the need and impulse for both coaches and teachers to create contrived lessons based on a preconceived idea of what defines good instruction for other classrooms. Rather, the more coaches practice, the more information they'll be able to integrate through the tasks of notice.

The more evidence coaches gather, the greater the ability to link that evidence to its effect on student learning.

Goal 5: Achieve Equity

Bilingual and dual-language teachers face a range of challenges in K–12 schools. They may receive less professional development and building-level systems of support, such as data meetings for bilingual and dual-language data, access to coaching, or involvement in PLCs. They may encounter unwritten language policies that negatively impact how effective bilingual and dual-language teachers appear, such as having to translate their lesson plans or only speak in English when coaches come to observe. They may also face inadequate or completely absent curricular materials designed for their bilingual and dual-language learners, among other issues (Linville, 2016; Pawan & Craig, 2011). When faced with such challenges, advocacy for greater equity in resources and supports for bilingual and dual-language teachers must be part of a coach's multidimensional role.

In addition to ensuring equity and access for bilingual and dual-language teachers, the observation and feedback cycle for every coach must also ensure equity and access for all students. Regardless of our ethnic background, we bring a cultural lens that impacts how we teach, perceive our students, and interpret what we see; it affects our willingness to change based on that interpretation. This cultural lens is a mix of memories, family traditions, places visited, languages, and people who have left their mark on who we are. Our beliefs about what we consider as normal behaviors, how we should teach, and how an environment supports academic success reflect our culture and subsequently shape the learning our students will experience. This lens also influences whether bilingual and dual-language teachers find and use texts that build on students' background knowledge, interpret certain student behaviors as aggressive or excited, or perceive students as lazy or slow rather than possibly being disconnected from a textbook that does not work for them.

This goal of equity for students acknowledges that even in bilingual and dual-language classrooms, there are times when the success of each and every student is not truly at the center of the teaching and learning process. Coaches must look for patterns of individuals or groups of students whose learning is not at the center of the teacher's planning and decision-making process.

To achieve equity, coaches require a certain level of courage to identify the lack of opportunity and the resulting lack of progress. Through this goal, coaches can also help set the tone and expectation for a teaching and learning community driven by shared responsibility for student success.

Goal 6: Incorporate Culture

The cultural context from which students, the school community, and the teacher come must also be a focus of coaches' work. How do teachers leverage their own and students' cultures in ways that honor their individual identities? Do they tap into them as powerful schema for adding new learning and incorporate them into the curriculum and classroom expectations? Coaches must consider these questions to validate students' identities, personalize learning, tap into students' background knowledge, and create powerful connections to content in the classroom. In my experience, when the classroom's collective culture truly incorporates students' individual cultures, I have seen powerful learning take place.

Just as is the case with any other coach, when I am observing a classroom, I bring with me who I am; I am never simply an observer. I bring my experience of having been a language learner, having taught language learners, and having observed and served teachers in a range of language learner structures. That range of experiences, both personal and professional, has led to a set of beliefs about what is important and effective. This includes a steadfast belief in using students' first language and personal reference points (or cultural and background knowledge) as invaluable resources and springboards for amazing and dynamic results in the classroom. Coaches who support teachers in bilingual and dual-language classrooms must embrace the research that supports tapping into and incorporating students' background knowledge and personal reference points as learning accelerators (Cummins, 2000).

Goal 7: Gather Accurate Evidence During the Observation

Not only must coaches ensure that all efforts of the observation and feedback cycle are focused on student learning, they must also make sure the cycle is based on observational evidence and gather that evidence with accuracy, validity, and consistency. Chapter 6 (page 71) is dedicated to helping coaches construct a more strategic understanding of the evidence collection process during the observation, applicable across all program goals and languages. There, I will present six tasks of notice vital to observational precision and strategic evidence collection: (1) environment and organization, (2) teacher-student interactions, (3) instructional strategies, (4) cause-and-effect relationships, (5) learning tasks, and (6) student agency over learning. For now, it is important to know that bilingual and dual-language teachers will gain greater trust in the accuracy of evidence collected during observation when employing these tasks of notice.

Goal 8: Embrace Best Practices

The greatest challenge for many monolingual coaches is to create an accurate model of effective bilingual and dual-language teacher practices that can lead to bilingualism and biliteracy, grade-level academic achievement, and sociocultural competence in their students. It requires that we suspend the existing schema and definition of effective instruction and best practice. Many coaches have not had significant opportunities to build a theoretical knowledge of sociocultural competency, second language acquisition, or those instructional strategies that create limitations or successes in students' content or language learning.

Will those differences in experience, however, limit our ability as coaches to see a true picture of what is taking place in the classroom? Prior knowledge of best practice can create problems for coaches as they begin to observe and provide feedback because, if left unchecked, observations are prone to many sources of error. A team of language educators determined, "You bring to the observation what you already believe" (Escamilla et al., 2013, p. 9).

Kathy Escamilla, project director of the Bilinguals United for Education and New Opportunities (BUENO) Center for Multicultural Education at the University of Colorado Boulder, has often discussed the challenges of accurately observing bilingual and dual-language students as they develop reading and writing skills. These challenges are due, in part, to the fact that these students are not simply engaged in the very complex process of learning to read. They also face further complications such as coming to a text with different background knowledge, decoding a different phonetic system, confronting an unfamiliar vocabulary, and applying the rules that differ from native language to second language. Coaches must adjust their analysis of bilingual and dual-language teachers' practices to account for additional strategies and consider a host of incredibly complex factors. As they collaborate with teachers to transform student outcomes, coaches must have a laser-like focus on research-based practices that are effective for bilingual and dual-language students and aligned to the particular model they are using.

This requires coaches to believe that good teaching is not the simple answer. Students do need good teachers, and there are some good universal teaching practices. However, the pedagogical and adaptive implications of learning a language while learning content always impact the learning experience. This means that bilingual and dual-language teachers who simply implement lessons with fidelity, as written in a textbook, won't often see the results promised by these lessons. Coaches need to be there to help teachers match those lessons with best practices for bilingual and dual-language learners. Coaches must prioritize helping bilingual and dual-language teachers embrace best practice over implementing curricular resources. However, coaches who take the time to first understand effective practices and then work to help teachers embrace and implement these practices are better able to leverage powerful opportunities for teachers to embed and seamlessly integrate language and culture with grade-level content.

Table 2.1 shows the empirically supported recommendations for the instructional strategies that define best practice for the language learning classroom. Furthermore, if fairness and student success are the guiding compass, coaches must prioritize these practices and should expect to find them integrated in all other content areas and used to support any purchased curricular resources.

Table 2.1: Practices and Approaches of Effective Bilingual and Dual-Language Programs

Model	Program Options	Effective and Best Practices	Prerequisites
English-only (L1 support is still provided as needed)	English language development (ELD), ESL, sheltered English instruction, structured English immersion (SEI)	Using native language strategically in explaining difficult concepts Teaching the components and processes of reading and writing to students who do not read in any language	Classroom organization; curriculum materials designed for language learners that can be adapted or supplemented to meet students' language, content, and cultural reference point needs
Bilingual	Bilingual, dual-language, two-way immersion, developmental bilingual, late exit, early exit, maintenance education heritage, transitional bilingual	1. Integrating strategic scaffolding and differentiation 2. Building and activating background knowledge 3. Teaching language through content and themes 4. Increasing emphasis on academic language development 5. Using data and formative assessment of academic language development in designing instruction and supports 6. Embedding cross-linguistic connections, which are a means of helping students see and analyze how languages function at the word, grammar, and sentence levels across the languages they are learning 7. Focusing on vocabulary development 8. Including explicit instructions that include models 9. Embracing interactive learning environments 10. Engaging in collaborative learning and reciprocal teaching for language and reading development	

continued →

Model	Program Options	Effective and Best Practices	Prerequisites
Bilingual	Bilingual, dual-language, two-way immersion, developmental bilingual, late exit, early exit, maintenance education heritage, transitional bilingual	11. Engaging students via culturally appropriate lessons and materials that reflect students' lives 12. Integrating instruction in reading, writing, listening, and speaking across the curriculum 13. Creating an academically language-rich classroom that includes visual aids 14. Including explicit oral language development 15. Offering feedback on content and academic language development and progress	Classroom organization; curriculum materials designed for language learners that can be adapted or supplemented to meet students' language, content, and cultural reference point needs

Source: August & Hakuta, 1997; August & Shanahan, 2006; Carlo et al., 2004; Genesee, Lindholm-Leary, Saunders, & Christian, 2006; Gersten et al., 2007; Klump & McNeir, 2005; Rivera et al., 2010; Short & Fitzsimmons, 2007; Thomas & Collier, 2012; Tivnan & Hemphill, 2005.

Regardless of the program model, the practices outlined in table 2.1 have the greatest influence on the achievement of bilingual and dual-language students and should be considered best practice. The empirical evidence about the impact of these practices for language learners must supersede the evidence available for what works with monolingual students.

Conclusion

In this chapter, we examined the goals of the observation and feedback cycle for coaches and teachers of bilingual and dual-language classrooms. There is no doubt that it requires effort for coaches to build their knowledge of the most effective practices for emergent bilinguals, but that effort can be eased by the belief that students and teachers in these classrooms are worth it. In many ways, this is simply what we would expect for coaches serving any other student group. In the next chapter, we explore the mindset coaches will need to adopt for a fair and effective observation and feedback cycle when they don't, or don't fully, speak the language of instruction.

Coaches can use the "Action-Planning Template" reproducible to help organize the learning from this chapter into smaller, more easily accomplished goals.

Chapter 2: Action-Planning Template

Use this chart to help you organize the learning from this chapter into smaller, more easily accomplished goals.

Next Steps	Time Line	Resources
1.		
2.		
3.		
4.		
5.		
6.		
7.		
8.		
9.		

Fair and Effective Feedback to Improve Teacher Practice

"Coaches and school leaders who do not speak the language of instruction really shouldn't be providing feedback to teachers, should they? That needs to be done by bilingual staff, right?" I've heard this concern expressed many times in my coaching career. This concern doesn't just come from coaches. I have heard bilingual teachers, bilingual leaders, postsecondary professors, researchers, and symposium panelists all express reactions ranging from curiosity to being adamant about the why nots of coaches not providing feedback if they are not proficient in the language of instruction or second language learning. I understand the hesitation, the challenge, and the very concerning history of feedback that causes educators to issue these cautionary warnings. I have also seen many coaches who look at the issue of feedback for bilingual and dual-language teachers with a strange mix of hesitation and false confidence.

There are four important things to remember about coaching and feedback.

1. All teachers deserve access to a system of supports designed to ensure their success and that of their students—it is a matter of social justice.
2. Coaching will play a critical role in creating road maps for how to improve the complex process of teaching and the equitable alignment of professional development.
3. The number of classrooms that reflect the cultural and linguistic complexity this book highlights have already exceeded the number of bilingual coaches and leaders available; and it's continuing to grow (Mitchell, 2019).
4. There are amazing coaches around the world who are already providing effective feedback that improves teacher practice and student achievement, even when they do not speak the languages of the classroom.

Being fluent in the language does help, but it isn't required to plot a clear path of improvement that builds a better educational future for students. We just have to be interested enough in the success of these students to adopt a process that improves how we support teachers. In doing so, we must acknowledge that fair and effective feedback may look a bit different when there's a language and cultural divide. So how is it different? What does it look like, sound like, and feel like? What are the characteristics of fair and effective feedback?

Characteristics of Fair and Effective Feedback

When it comes to providing feedback that leads to improvement, coaches must have a clear understanding of the characteristics of fair and effective feedback. In the context of bilingual and dual-language classrooms, new characteristics of fair feedback will need to replace previously held ideas and assumptions. However, these four characteristics will remain the same: (1) understanding the role of feedback, (2) leading and leveraging emotional intelligence, (3) taking an inquiry stance, and (4) using well-developed problem-solving skills.

When it comes to coaching, feedback is sharing information with teachers after an observation in order to determine which changes in the decision-making process are most likely to improve student learning outcomes. Feedback is defined by a reaction or response by the coach to what he or she observed in the classroom and then analyzed after the fact. Feedback is also characterized by how systematically it works to improve teaching and student outcomes. For example, when the teacher poses a question or presents a strategy (instructional decision), does it help students acquire more complex academic language and content mastery than before (language and learning outcomes)?

However, fair feedback should not include the coach's *opinions* about things like strategies the teacher uses, the necessity of using another language as an instructional tool, or the exchange of language and learning goals to keep all teachers consistent in their practice. We all have opinions and beliefs. We are human beings, after all. These beliefs only become problematic when those about content, instruction, outcomes, and resources are so strong that a coach might forget and sometimes even reject the additional content and language teachers must plan for. Allowing beliefs and opinions to influence feedback can increase the number of instructional decisions that coaches miss in these classrooms. Alternatively, placing boundaries around opinions helps focus feedback on improving the accuracy of each instructional decision to improve student learning outcomes.

Fair feedback is value-free feedback. Coaches must resist the urge to evaluate teachers and their instructional decisions as right or wrong, good or bad, or valuable or futile. Feedback like, "I really liked when . . . " or "You're wasting time on . . . when you should be . . . " increases the likelihood of conversations becoming emotionally charged. Coaches must develop an awareness of their own biases that helps manage the ebb and flow of conversations with the goal of making people change. This self-awareness requires a certain amount of emotional intelligence in communicating information and making adjustments in the moment. Even though most educators want to see themselves as reflective, change is hard. Coaches can overcome this challenge by being hyper-aware of what they are feeling in the moment and using that information to make necessary shifts that keep the thinking and inquiry process productive (Goleman, 1995).

Do not confuse the need to reflect on and manage personal opinions with avoiding difficult conversations. On the contrary, coaches must never shy away from challenging conversations; they just need to approach them with the goal of maintaining a student-centered and productive conversation that leads to positive outcomes.

Coaches should set specific goals when giving feedback. They should explore, monitor, and refine those goals before possible feedback traps derail their efforts. Table 3.1 (page 42) shows some of the traps coaches might experience.

Classrooms are complex spaces. However, classrooms that serve culturally and linguistically diverse students, especially in another language, add an infinite amount of complexity, possible turning points, and potential paths forward. Coaches require a great deal of qualitative data, quantitative data, and common sense to be able to accurately recommend any one path forward. Qualitative data will come from the tasks of notice, or structured protocols for coaches to observe bilingual and dual-language classrooms to collect accurate and consistent data (see chapter 6, page 71, for more detailed information) completed during the observation. Quantitative data must come from various types of formative and summative literacy, language, and content assessments.

Finally, common sense must lead coaches to ask open, high-quality questions that result in meaningful dialogue with teachers. Each instructional moment that a coach observes represents a myriad of possible turning points to explore. The coach committed to fair and effective feedback will value the insights that EL, DL, and TBE teachers can offer. For that reason, they should work together to explore the factors, underlying issues, or misconceptions that might contribute to students not fully realizing their success.

Table 3.1: Feedback Goals and Traps

Feedback Goals	Feedback Traps
Give and show respect.	The coach points out specific issues, efforts, and signs of progress, but does not do so in a respectful manner. This can result in teachers being less likely to put forth the energy to address these opportunities to improve their practice.
Nurture the connection and relationship with teachers before providing feedback for improvement.	There is no replacement for authentic connections. Some bilingual and dual-language teachers might feel offended and disrespected by coaches who simply jump in and tell them what to do.
Know what you want and why.	The coach includes asides that are not in the best interest for language learners; rather, they are in the best interest of a new initiative.
Don't avoid difficult conversations.	The coach avoids unpleasant conversations because they can impact the relationship. However, if every student matters, then coaches cannot avoid conversations at the expense of a fair and effective educational experience.
Keep your options open unless the rights and dignities of students are at stake.	Thinking that there is only one way forward insults the complex work teachers do and lessens your credibility as a provider of well-thought-out feedback and options.
Assess which approach you'll need to take based on your goals and teachers' current skills and wills.	Coaches use the same approach all the time, regardless of the teacher or the complexity of the classroom. Coaches must recognize that all teachers are different. As such, coaches must have a range of methods and approaches for the diverse teachers they serve in order to maintain a constructive conversation that leads to action and continuous improvement.
Acknowledge, advocate, and collaboratively work to remove real barriers.	Teachers who serve EL, DL, and TBE students constantly face barriers to equity, access, and resources. These barriers are rarely the only things preventing teachers from moving their practice forward. It is the coach's job to acknowledge the barrier, advocate against the barrier, and push past the barrier to support the teacher.
Get feedback about the impact and success of coaching sessions.	Coaches can easily trap themselves in the role of expert. Feedback should be a two-way street. When they don't create a structured space for feedback from the teachers they serve, they can get trapped into a false sense of confidence about their efficacy.
Prioritize what matters most—the one essential question that moves the work forward—one at a time.	Coaches try to tackle too much at once. No one can master all things simultaneously. Coaches should prioritize feedback to focus on specific items for improvement that teachers can work on and master.
Ask powerful questions and then get out of the way and listen.	Coaches can sometimes give too many answers and suggestions instead of allowing teachers to co-construct their own path forward. If you own the answers to your questions, you also own the results (good or bad). If you don't ask good questions, teachers won't discover good answers that improve student learning.

Source: Adapted from Kaye & Jordan-Evans, 2003.

Teachers and coaches can transfer many of the methods and techniques used in monolingual observation and feedback processes to the bilingual and dual-language classroom. Coaches will benefit from any prior coaching experience as they work to provide bilingual and dual-language teachers with feedback that teachers can understand and apply to improve practice, increase student learning, and strengthen their problem-solving abilities (Hattie, 2012).

Transparency in Feedback

The process for fairly and effectively observing and providing feedback in a bilingual and dual-language classroom where the coach does not speak the language requires a unique process distinct from the one most educators use. We have already discussed why a different process is necessary for bilingual and dual-language classrooms if it is to result in consistently accurate feedback that leads to improved student learning. Since the process will be different from what teachers have experienced in the past, bilingual and dual-language teachers who are new to this observation and feedback cycle with coaches who don't speak the language of instruction will need time to understand the process and why it should be trusted.

This process transparency should include the specific steps that the observation and feedback cycle entails. Coaches should let teachers know that the process is not meant to be prescriptive even though it will follow a very predictable structure. Instead of having a fixed formula for things like what each lesson must look like and how teachers must allocate their time, or identifying the exact ingredients of each small-group activity, we should define the effectiveness of the coaching cycle by how well coach and teacher can work together to note critical turning points of a lesson. Coach and teacher should both be able to jointly examine the impact of those turning points and collaborate on an evidence-based course of action that maps out the supports necessary to make the changes that yield greater learning for all students (Bryk, Gomez, Grunow, & Lemahieu, 2015).

At the core of the nonprescriptive approach is understanding the ever-growing and complex web of knowledge, skills, and abilities bilingual and dual-language teachers need to effectively coordinate instructional experiences in bilingual and dual-language classrooms. Communicating this approach through words, actions, and collaboration is the best way for coaches to support the observation and feedback cycle. Coaches who have taken the time to become an insider, not an outsider may consider trying out or practicing some of the tasks of notice for no more than one or two minutes during these early visits. The extra practice will lead to greater accuracy. And as coaches share with teachers the aspects of a lesson they find effective in their classroom visits with greater accuracy, teachers begin to see firsthand just how accurate this cycle can be.

Conclusion

This chapter explored how to define a fair system of feedback focused on students. Coaches will be able to leverage many of the skills they already use in providing feedback to teachers in other fields. However, they must be cautious of the feedback traps that can derail their efforts and hard work. The next chapter takes these tools and strategies and explores the mindset shift needed to frame the foundation for and effectively engage in the full observation and feedback cycle with bilingual and dual-language teachers.

Coaches can use the "Action-Planning Template" reproducible to help organize the learning from this chapter into smaller, more easily accomplished goals.

Chapter 3: Action-Planning Template

Use this chart to help you organize the learning from this chapter into smaller, more easily accomplished goals.

Next Steps	Time Line	Resources
1.		
2.		
3.		
4.		
5.		
6.		
7.		
8.		
9.		

Part 2

The Observation and Feedback Cycle

Mindset Essentials That Frame the Foundation for the Observation and Feedback Cycle

The observation and feedback cycle presented in this book is unique from those experienced by many bilingual and dual-language teachers and the coaches who serve them. Even still, there is an essential shift in mindset that coaches will need to undergo and that serves as the first stage in the observation and feedback cycle for bilingual and dual-language teachers. Through this shift in mindset, the coach will have the opportunity to create the foundation that is necessary for the full process of observation and feedback for bilingual and dual-language teachers to be effective.

Coaches must create a foundation for this cycle if it's to have any chance of realizing its potential. Figure 4.1 (page 50) shows the four stages of the observation and feedback cycle.

In creating a solid foundation for the observation and feedback cycle, coaches should strive to develop seven mindset essentials. These seven mindset essentials include: (1) establish trust and confidence; (2) avoid hidden agendas; (3) lead by learning; (4) become an insider, not an outsider; (5) know the right things; (6) ensure confidentiality; and (7) know when to use spotlights and supports. Once coaches are clear on the eight goals of the coaching process, as described in chapter 2 (page 23), they are better able to approach this shift in mindset. This mindset shift is an important part of the observation and feedback cycle that frames the pre-observation conference with bilingual and dual-language teachers.

1. Establish trust and confidence.
2. Avoid hidden agendas.
3. Lead by learning.
4. Become an insider, not an outsider.
5. Know the right things.
6. Ensure confidentiality.
7. Know when to use spotlights and supports.

STAGE 1
Mindset essentials that frame the foundation

STAGE 2
Pre-observation conference

STAGE 3
Observation (six tasks of notice and four essential questions)

STAGE 4
Post-observation conference

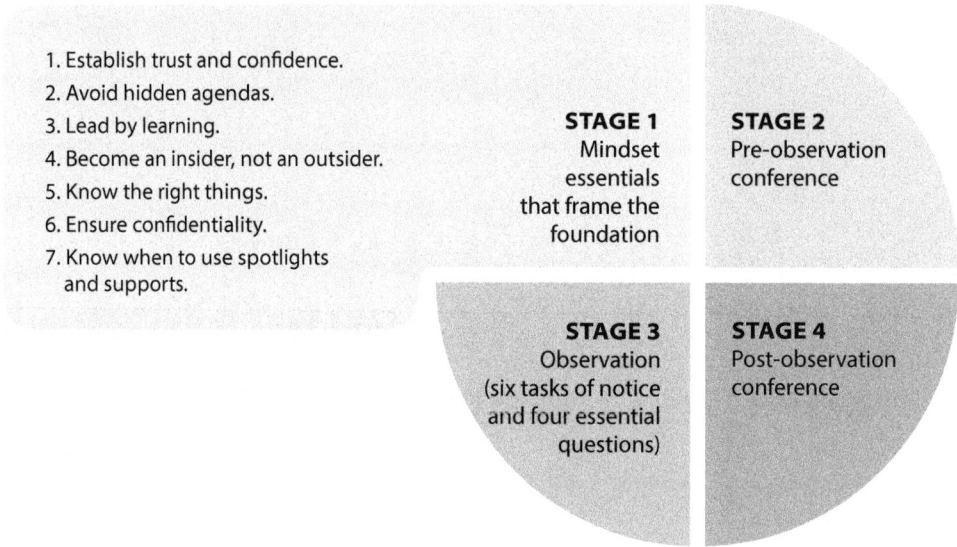

Figure 4.1: Four stages of the observation and feedback cycle.

Establish Trust and Confidence

Trust is an essential characteristic of any successful coaching relationship. Without it, bilingual and dual-language teachers will never feel comfortable enough to have open and honest conversations about areas for improvement. Much like the language learners they serve, bilingual and dual-language teachers need emotional safety and confidence to take the risks inherent in collaboration, reflection, and negotiating changes in practice.

Coaches must earn the trust of the teachers they work with. Coaches who do not speak languages other than English will most likely have to work harder at building confidence. I've noticed that many bilingual and dual-language teachers are suspicious of this process and expect to be misunderstood. And while no person should have to pay for the missteps and mistakes of other coaches or administrators, the reality is that each coach needs to approach his or her initial interactions and pre-observation conferences with a high level of emotional intelligence and sensitivity.

Avoid Hidden Agendas

Stephen R. Covey (1989) discusses the idea of a shared goal or underlying agenda in his fourth habit of highly effective people. This win-win agreement between coach and teacher is equally important to both if the relationship is going to move teaching practice forward. Coaches must be intentional about how they frame their agenda, or plan, and in what ways it will be similar to or different from past experiences, other classrooms, and other approaches to coaching. The teachers they work with must believe there are no hidden agendas that might diminish or devalue their work. By sharing their agendas, coaches can create credibility through transparency.

Lead by Learning

Before the first coaching cycle, coaches should take the time to assume the role of a learner. Coaches who serve bilingual and dual-language teachers must be comfortable and flexible enough to understand what defines these classrooms and how these theories, practices, and bodies of research are coordinated to ensure student success. They should learn about their bilingual and dual-language teachers, their students, the assessments that drive instruction, and the unique ways these classrooms operate in a complex world of content, language, and culture.

Being a learner doesn't have to be a structured and fixed role. Sometimes it is about asking critical questions, listening with an open mind, and choosing to suspend any preconceived ideas of what is right or wrong. It might also involve reviewing language proficiency data with teachers to learn the complex process each student must follow to become proficient in each language they are working to acquire. This small shift allows coaches to recognize bilingual and dual-language teachers for the knowledge they bring to their craft before asking to serve learners.

Become an Insider, Not an Outsider

The most important learning happens when coaches visit classrooms where teaching and learning are taking place in the LOTE. This means that coaches who take the time to visit bilingual and dual-language classrooms allow a level of exposure that shifts their mindsets to the cadence of bilingual and dual-language lessons and the ways that language, culture, and content constantly depend on one another as the norms in these classrooms. This shift happens for a number of reasons. First, coaches are usually linguistic outsiders in bilingual and dual-language classrooms, especially those who don't fully understand the language of instruction. Often, teachers and students in these bilingual and dual-language settings form a close bond as a result of the language and cultural connection that is not typically found in monolingual classrooms. When coaches who don't share that language and culture bond enter into that space, it is easy for students to lose focus on the lesson because of curiosity about the visit from someone who is not a part of that family-like bond. In most cases, this harmless curiosity fades after students see a coach as a regular visitor who is genuinely interested in their learning, even if he or she doesn't understand the language.

Coaches also need to spend time acclimating to the standard operating procedures in these classrooms. An accurate picture of effective teaching can only happen when instruction is delivered in the language regularly used for each content area. This means that if coaches require observations to be done in English only (or any other language that the coach knows), they may get the impression that students are unengaged or don't like to participate because students aren't responding as they typically would due to this switch. Coaches can become insiders, with greater influence in the observation and feedback cycle, by taking time to understand what the program model and pedagogical approaches look like and sound like in action, and identify how the teachers are leveraging and celebrating culture to improve student confidence and achievement in these classrooms.

Know the Right Things

Teachers and schools must trust coaches to admit what they don't know. Being strategically vulnerable is okay. It shows that coaches are not trying to pretend to be an expert at everything. It also allows the coaching relationship to be a more balanced partnership in which each person knows what expertise the other brings to the table.

On the other hand, if coaches take this idea too far and only communicate their lack of knowledge and personal experience in the LOTE or the curriculum, instruction, and assessment work that define the program, it will be challenging to get bilingual and dual-language teachers to see how they or their students benefit from engaging in the observation and feedback cycle. Coaches must be clear on what they know and don't know and how this knowledge can help the teachers they work with better serve their students. Minimally, coaches must know to simultaneously focus their feedback on growing language and achievement, analyzing how interactional trends cause specific student results, building in more professional development and supports that speak to the needs of their bilingual and dual-language learners, and advocating for the needs of bilingual and dual-language students. These are the right things (which are developed more fully in chapter 6, page 71) that coaches must be able to articulate with confidence if they want to show teachers they have the credibility necessary to do this work.

Ensure Confidentiality

Another critical element of the framework is confidentiality. If bilingual and dual-language teachers are to trust their coaches and share information about barriers that might be standing in the way of student learning, they must know that any information they share is confidential and private. Coaches should explicitly address the issue of confidentiality before any observation or visit in a bilingual and dual-language classroom.

Know When to Use Spotlights and Supports

There are two exceptions to the confidentiality rule. The first exception is when a coach observes a lesson or practice that yields such good results that it begs him or her to shine a spotlight and share it with other educators in the same program. Even though this break in confidentiality is for the purpose of appreciation, recognition, and celebration, it still represents a break in the coaching agreement, and as such, requires the coach to first obtain permission from the teacher. Sharing powerful practices, resources, linguistic scaffolds, and successful lessons is vital to sustaining a bilingual and dual-language program so we can replicate successes without burning out teachers who already spend countless hours creating visuals and language activities, translating, finding culturally authentic materials, and so on. Coaches might also want to share effective practices and resources with the broader monolingual staff so everyone sees that they, too, share responsibility for the success of all language learners.

The second exception is when a coach needs to discuss an observation with a specialist. Support networks can help guide new coaches by giving context and insight into aspects of the observation that may be outside of a coach's expertise and understanding, such as teaching grounded in the second language acquisition process or student culture. Understanding this context is critical for coaches, as it helps them be more accurate in their interpretations and insights. Further, it shows teachers that coaches are committed to understanding more than prescribing, and that their agenda is truly about teacher and student success. Like the first exception, this requires coaches to receive permission from teachers in order to discuss what they have observed so as not to break the sense of trust established between teacher and coach.

Conclusion

This chapter explored how to shift one's mindset in order to ensure that the observation and feedback cycle is one that is fair and focused on the set goals. Coaches will need to apply this shift in mindset in each stage of the observation and feedback cycle. The next chapter takes these mindset shifts and applies them to engaging in the pre-observation conference with bilingual and dual-language teachers.

Coaches can use the "Action-Planning Template" reproducible (page 54) to help organize the learning from this chapter into smaller, more easily accomplished goals.

Chapter 4: Action-Planning Template

Use this chart to help you organize the learning from this chapter into smaller, more easily accomplished goals.

Next Steps	Time Line	Resources
1.		
2.		
3.		
4.		
5.		
6.		
7.		
8.		
9.		

CHAPTER 5

The Pre-Observation Conference

The pre-observation conference is the second stage in the observation and feedback cycle for bilingual and dual-language teachers. Through the pre-observation conference, the teacher and coach will have the opportunity to collaboratively learn what the process will entail, speak frankly about how they will work together to overcome the language barrier, and prove to each other that this is a relationship and partnership worth investing in. While the coach comes into this pre-observation conference with a range of things he or she needs to discuss, both the coach and teacher must negotiate the rule and norms for the conference.

Figure 5.1 (page 56) shows how the pre-observation conference fits into the observation and feedback cycle, along with the nine elements essential to this stage in the process.

The pre-observation conference is an important part of the observation and feedback cycle. It provides coaches with much-needed insight into teachers' intentionality in instruction design. Coaches will struggle to maximize the observation and feedback cycle if they don't fully understand the strengths and opportunities in teachers' thinking and the intentionality of their design process, which consists of unique steps in the pre-observation process. Yet, the perceived strengths and opportunities a coach identifies in a teacher's planning process are just the start of the plan for the full observation and feedback cycle. Coaches also need to thoroughly grasp the importance of interdependent factors (further described in chapter 6, page 71), such as how teachers implement that plan or how they adjust that plan in the moment to improve students' learning.

Many coaches with experience supporting monolingual teachers will need time to consider adjustments and adaptations to the typical questions they are used to asking, which don't take culture, language, dual-language-specific strategies,

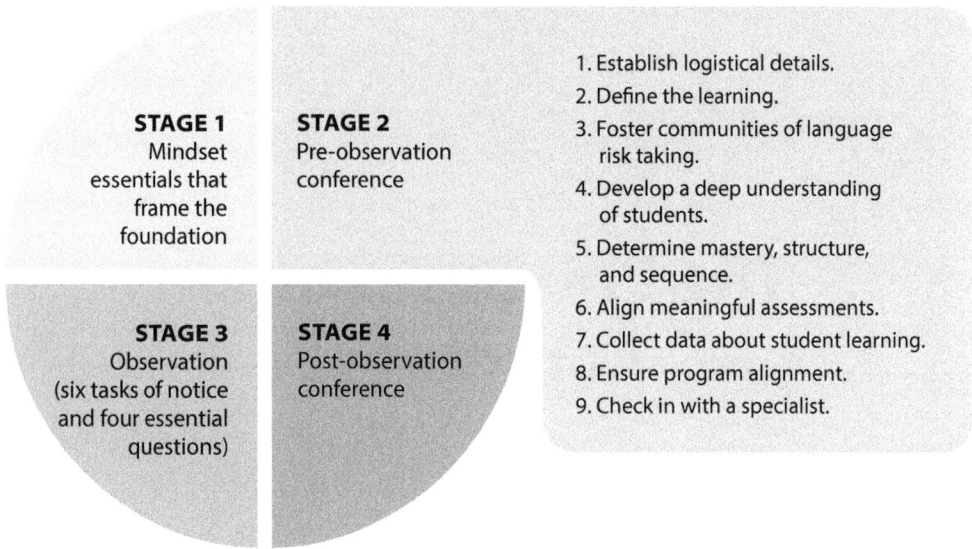

		1. Establish logistical details.
STAGE 1	STAGE 2	2. Define the learning.
Mindset	Pre-observation	3. Foster communities of language
essentials that	conference	risk taking.
frame the		4. Develop a deep understanding
foundation		of students.
		5. Determine mastery, structure,
STAGE 3	STAGE 4	and sequence.
Observation	Post-observation	6. Align meaningful assessments.
(six tasks of notice	conference	7. Collect data about student learning.
and four essential		8. Ensure program alignment.
questions)		9. Check in with a specialist.

Figure 5.1: Nine elements of the pre-observation conference.

and so on, into account. The adaptations to the guiding questions in this chapter represent augmented considerations that should guide coaches' thinking around the instructional design process. These adapted guiding questions indicate what coaches need to analyze with bilingual and dual-language teachers in order to understand the complex intersections of content, language, and cultural learning that these teachers must design. Without using these guiding questions, the pre-observation conference does little to improve the observation and feedback process. The guiding questions allow coaches to develop a more accurate picture of the relationship among planning, instructional delivery, and in-the-moment instructional changes and student learning in bilingual and dual-language classrooms.

Coaches will find that adjustments to their typical process (to include aspects of culture, language, and dual-language-specific strategies) help provide much-needed clarity to the interactions they will observe in another language. The pre-observation conference considerations presented in figure 5.1 and further explained in this chapter provide greater structure and focus to this conference in order to improve the ways coaches and bilingual and dual-language teachers plan a process that incorporates language, literacy, content, and culture.

In addition, the guiding questions can sometimes point out during a pre-observation conference when a teacher's beliefs or thinking need adjustment as well. This could include thinking that disputes students' ability to learn at high levels, thinking that approaches instructional planning with a one-size-fits-all mentality, or thinking that argues against the use of certain instructional strategies that conflict with personal beliefs, like cross-linguistic connections or translanguaging.

There are a lot of misconceptions about translanguaging. Ricardo Otheguy, Ofelia García, and Wallis Reid (2015) define *translanguaging* as "the deployment of a speaker's full linguistic repertoire without regard for watchful adherence to the socially and politically defined boundaries of . . . languages" (p. 281). In short, translanguaging allows bilingual and dual-language students to show the full extent of what they know and are able to do. Teachers can promote this practice by allowing students to use both languages while maintaining a watchful adherence to what students are saying in one language or another. This allows students to fully communicate their thinking, even if that means code switching, while giving teachers greater information about students' language boundaries. *Code switching* is when students move between different languages, dialects, or registers as they produce language, such as between English, Spanish, academic language, and slang as they work on a project in class.

Rather than continue to the next set of guiding questions, coaches should feel comfortable in pausing from what they'd planned for the pre-observation conference to ask bilingual and dual-language teachers about when they will insist on students staying in one language and when they will allow them to tap into both languages in real time.

The guiding questions offered in the following sections are not a checklist of questions that coaches must ask. Nor should coaches read them verbatim. Instead, coaches should use these guiding questions to guide their own thinking process as they conference with teachers. Allow the quality of the pre-observation conference itself to drive the questions.

Establish Logistical Details

The first step in the pre-observation conference is for coaches and teachers to simply coordinate the details of the lesson to be observed. Coaches will want to clarify items like the date and time, what class they will observe, what program model the teacher uses in that class, the grade level or grade levels (since it is common for bilingual and dual-language teachers to teach more than one level per classroom), and even where in the classroom they should sit to minimize interruption. Coaches are often surprised to learn just how many bilingual and dual-language teachers teach multiple grades, multiple groups or sections, and multiple languages. This is critical background information that will help contextualize the instructional design to be discussed. Coaches will want to discuss the following logistical details.

- **Self-contained or side-by-side program model:** This provides coaches with greater clarity regarding the composition of the program. In a *self-contained program*, one teacher delivers all core content and language instruction. That one teacher is responsible for both languages. In a *side-by-side model*, two teachers work together (side by side) to plan and coordinate instruction and cross-linguistic connections across the two languages. The LOTE bilingual and dual-language teacher teaches some of the content in one language, and the English bilingual and dual-language teacher teaches the other content in English.
- **A/B schedules:** This clarifies the schedule used in a particular DLL model. Many side-by-side programs have alternating schedules in which the letters *A* and *B* represent groups of students; some use different colors instead of letters. These two classrooms might alternate schedules in the morning or afternoon or day by day. For example, group A would go to their Spanish DLL teacher in the morning and then go to their English DLL teacher in the afternoon. Group B would have the exact opposite schedule.
- **Push-in or pull-out model:** This clarifies where the bilingual and dual-language teachers provide instruction. In the *push-in* model, teachers instruct students while they are still inside of their general education classroom settings, as is the case with co-teaching models. In the *pull-out* model, teachers remove students from the general education classroom to deliver instruction in a separate location. This is often how teachers coordinate instruction when there are students from many different language backgrounds in various classrooms.
- **Native language groupings:** This clarifies how teachers use students' first languages to group them. For example, some DLL programs intentionally group students by their native languages in order to coordinate language development supports. Other DLL programs organize their reading interventions by native language or first language (L1).

Define the Learning

Coaches who work with bilingual and dual-language teachers must be clear about what students are learning—the goal of the lesson. Why are students there? What are they to learn? Why is that particular learning goal the right thing for each student to learn at that particular time? And what will be the most effective and evidence-based approach to accelerate every student's learning? These questions highlight why goals must remain at the forefront of the pre-observation conference. The answers to these questions reveal glimpses into the teacher's thinking about other components of the instructional design process.

Coaches can use the guiding questions in figure 5.2, and the remaining guiding questions and templates, to help them organize their thoughts for the pre-observation conference. Coaches should feel free to add any questions they feel are necessary to help them understand teachers' instructional decisions.

Guiding Questions	What are the goals for this lesson?
	How did you plan for the content and language objectives? How did you determine literacy development that is authentic to the languages of literacy and cultural backgrounds of the class?
	How do you address the Common Core State Standards, state standards, language development standards, and cultural proficiency standards within the instructional design?
	Why are these the correct objectives for the range of language proficiency levels?
	How did you ensure that these goals don't repeat learning that students have already mastered during their time in the other program language (specific to dual-language classrooms)?
Look-fors	
Reflections	

Figure 5.2: Guiding questions, look-fors, and reflections to define learning.

*Visit **go.SolutionTree.com/EL** for a free reproducible version of this figure.*

The look-fors section of the template gives coaches a place to identify what practices or teacher moves they should be aware of and alert to during the observation even without knowing the language of instruction. Coaches can complete the look-fors section with teachers during the pre-observation conference. They should also feel free to include responses by the teacher that highlight his or her thinking for this guiding question.

Lastly, coaches should use the reflections section immediately after the conclusion of the pre-observation conference to identify any areas that need clarification with a specialist (see Check in With a Specialist, page 66). This reflection will help coaches identify questions that still remain. Coaches can also use this section to pre-identify and record the connections between the pre-observation conference and teacher evaluation, if the observation will be included in that teacher's evaluation. While there is never enough time in the day, coaches must try to engage in this reflection as quickly as possible. I have found that the reflection stage increases the consistency and legitimacy of the observation and feedback cycle for teachers and boosts the accuracy and confidence of the feedback for coaches. When completed, the template represents a concrete picture of the teacher's instructional design process in action.

Foster Communities of Language Risk Taking

An essential aspect of bilingual and dual-language classrooms is that coaches often find they need to build teachers' capacity and willingness to continually help students increase the amount of language they are able to understand, use, and produce, giving them access to more content and experiences in that language. However, this requires language learners to venture beyond the comfort of what they already know how to do so they can try out new words, language structures, and tasks, which are never perfect the first time around. Mistakes can be very daunting, but effective bilingual and dual-language teachers intentionally design ways to encourage students' confidence, build their self-esteem, and empower them to own their learning. Because of this, teachers are often hesitant to push more advanced academic vocabulary and language structures.

Coaches can help teachers build this language rigor by making sure teachers encourage students to use two key phrases as they try new things: "I need help" and "Can you explain that again?" These teachers must continually design ways to bring diverse students, needs, and backgrounds into one community that honors and values everyone's culture, where each individual feels safe enough to take the risks inherent in making mistakes.

Figure 5.3 offers guiding questions to foster communities of language risk taking in the classroom.

Develop a Deep Understanding of Students

In order to effectively teach students, teachers must know their students. They must know their strengths, their needs, and how they learn best, among other factors. While bilingual and dual-language teachers need to know how students are performing in mathematics and reading, these high-stakes, English-only tests don't account for students' developing language proficiency and provide teachers an incomplete picture of who their students are and how to best meet their needs. Instead, bilingual and dual-language teachers need to use a different approach to student assessment and incorporate those data into a broader picture of each student.

Effective assessments for bilingual and dual-language students differ from traditional assessments in three key ways: (1) language proficiency data influence the

Guiding Questions	What have you done to encourage participation and continual language growth for all students, even those who have recently arrived? How have you been able to balance students' individual needs and identities with building a strong community? Do all students step out of their comfort zone to try new ways of applying content and using language?
Look-fors	
Reflections	

Figure 5.3: Guiding questions, look-fors, and reflections to foster communities of language risk taking.

Visit **go.SolutionTree.com/EL** *for a free reproducible version of this figure.*

instructional design process, (2) teachers assess and use home language and literacy as tools to accelerate the English development process, and (3) more descriptive student profiles provide robust reference points that teachers must consider when diagnosing low or minimal progress.

The influence of language proficiency on instructional design is one of the most important differences. Research on how second languages are acquired offers clear guidance on applying the information from language proficiency assessments to better meet the needs of students and improve their outcomes (August & Shanahan, 2006; WIDA Consortium, 2010). Simply using the information learned from language proficiency assessments is not enough, though. If teachers use assessments to deeply understand the students they serve, then they need access to valid and reliable assessments for all subject-area learning that also take into account the interconnections of language and literacy development and their impact on subject-area learning.

If bilingual and dual-language teachers are going to use these elements to coordinate the most effective instructional design, then coaches must help them understand how assessments (such as formative, summative, diagnostic, and linguistically modified) inform the way they present content, use scaffolds, decide on texts, and create opportunities to apply new learning in meaningful and accessible ways. Coaches must also look for aspects of the pre-observation conference that address grouping, achievement of content and language goals, the need for intervention, and students' progress in language development.

Bilingual and dual-language teachers need something that few other teachers in the building need: access to more accurate, authentic, and usable information about their students' literacy and learning in their native languages. Each dual-language program leverages a specific approach and strategy for the ways it uses students' two languages at different points (for example, using strategies to make cross-linguistic connections, translanguaging, or encouraging and reinforcing the use of the language of instruction) in order to achieve more advanced levels of literacy in both languages.

As part of the pre-observation conference, coaches must not shy away from an open and inquiry-based conversation about how and why teachers use each language when they're developing print literacy. The goal is for coaches to understand how teachers strategically address the long-term literacy skills students need to read, think critically about, comprehend, and communicate that comprehension across two languages. Coaches must be closely tuned into any assessment or data analysis protocols unique to these classrooms and vital to progress monitoring, interventions, and accelerations in both languages. This is especially the case if this coaching is the teachers' only support in analyzing the information learned from these assessments.

More intentional and strategic use of assessments provides much-needed information for bilingual and dual-language teachers to help in the instructional design process, and teachers will need coaches who are willing to help them navigate multiple data points specific to the bilingual and dual-language classroom. Teachers need to know what makes each student unique and what it takes to ensure his or her success. This knowledge helps teachers move beyond seeing their students as mere numbers to understanding their stories, backgrounds, values, and more. Many teachers have forged relationships with their students for their own personal reasons; maybe because they see young versions of themselves in their students, or perhaps they feel a maternal or paternal urge to care for students who might just need a little extra compassion and understanding. More than anything, bilingual and dual-language teachers work to help students feel comfortable and safe so they can trust adults enough to lower their *affective filter*, defined by Stephen Krashen (1987) as an emotional guard that can either block students from all learning or open up students to learning and language use, depending on the level of emotional distress and anxiety levels they experience.

Table 5.1 lists factors that impact the success of language learners, which bilingual and dual-language teachers must take into account when they are striving to understand and learn more about their students.

Table 5.1: Factors That Impact the Success of Language Learners

Factors That Offer a Deep Understanding of Students	Sources
Learning Conditions	• Teachers • Resources and access to needed services • Program model and implementation • The role of home language and home culture • The role of assessment on instructional design
Academic Success and Quality of Instruction	• Means by which students show what they know in each content area • Evidence-based strategies for coaches to support teachers in promoting students' language proficiency and academic achievement • Identification of students' knowledge and application of content rather than invalid inferences based on language proficiency and literacy levels
Oral Language Development and Native Language Literacy	• First language experiences • Print literacy in students' home language • Literacy support at home, with another caregiver, or entrusted guardian that speaks to how well the learning environment gives each culturally and linguistically diverse student the opportunity to learn (Gee, 2008)
Quality of Second Language Literacy Instruction	• Literacy instruction in English that does or does not prioritize context, background knowledge, visuals, frontloading, and discussion • Development of reading vocabulary in context, not in isolation • The level of literacy attained in the home language • Reinforcement of literacy support at home
Physical and Psychological Factors	• Medical conditions and illness • Health (dental, vision, hearing) • Nutrition and access to food • Ability to access treatment for health conditions • Mental health (depression, anxiety, or other issues) • Social and emotional development • Sense of belonging to the school and community
Personal and Family Factors	• Family dynamics, expectations, and aspirations • Social and emotional development • Socioeconomic status • Parental engagement • Student interest • Experiential background
Previous Schooling	• Exposure to and mastery of standards needed for success in the current year • Provision of instructional approach and supports, interventions, and accelerations • Progression of language development and language chunks that allows access to the current grade-level curriculum
Dual Cultures	• Connection of students' background knowledge with emphasis on the value of knowledge learned in the home and community • Connection between adults' valuation and use of cultural and linguistic resources and what students already know to attain high academic achievement and language development (Harry, Kalyanpur, & Day, 1999; Harry, Rueda, & Kalyanpur, 1999; Warger, 2001)

Source: Adapted from WIDA Consortium, 2013.

*Visit **go.SolutionTree.com/EL** for a free reproducible version of this table.*

The factors listed in table 5.1 (page 63) should inform teachers' efforts to deeply understand the students they serve, since these factors provide insight into what bilingual and dual-language students need to be successful. When teachers leverage a combination of information learned from assessments and non-assessment sources (such as interviews, parent meetings, and introductory activities), they are better equipped to design instruction that results in successful learning experiences.

Figure 5.4 offers coaches guiding questions that can help them to prepare teachers to use the complex information they've gathered to improve their instruction and understand how well it connects content, language learning, and cultural relevancy.

Guiding Questions	How have you adapted instruction for students with additional factors impacting their success? What are those factors?
	In what ways does your classroom mirror the cultural norms and sensitivities of your students?
	Who is the most challenging student in the class, and what supports are currently in place that address the individual factors that contribute to the challenge?
	Were there any school rules that you had to help students negotiate, and how did you do that while honoring their identity?
	Have you identified any cultural or linguistic challenges for your students, and how have you addressed those challenges?
	How did you plan for participation by English learners early in their language-learning journey?
	How have you built in time for intentional oral language practice, and how does it help your academic goals?
	How have you tapped into your families as partners to support your students' success?
	How do you organize all the information you've learned about your students so you are able to recognize critical data points in a single view?
Look-fors	
Reflections	

Figure 5.4: Guiding questions, look-fors, and reflections to develop a deep understanding of students.

*Visit **go.SolutionTree.com/EL** for a free reproducible version of this figure.*

Determine Mastery, Structure, and Sequence; Align Meaningful Assessments; and Collect Data About Student Learning

Coaches will notice that explicit attention is missing to guiding questions five through seven in the pre-observation conference:

- Determine mastery, structure, and sequence
- Align meaningful assessments
- Collect data about student learning

The absence of explicit guiding questions, look-fors, and reflections is not an indication that discussing these guiding questions during the pre-observation conference is not important. Rather, significant time has already been dedicated to exploring the implications of assessing and using assessment data as part of the instructional design process. Since part 1 of this book and this chapter have already examined the role and use of assessments, the rest of this chapter will address those final guiding questions that coaches must learn to adjust in order to maximize the coaching cycle.

Ensure Program Alignment

Just as is the case with every student, every teacher, and even every subject area, every bilingual and dual-language program is different. Each has its own unique set of goals, with a distinct vision for developing language proficiency and academic success that requires consistency in the application of methods and practices from one year to the next. The goals and vision of success held by each program determine which instructional practices are or are not appropriate. Consider program alignment the equivalent of seeing a Bunsen burner in a kindergarten classroom rather than a high school science class. I am pretty sure that I would panic if I saw a Bunsen burner in a classroom for five-year-olds, even if it wasn't turned on! In the appropriate context, however, I'm excited to see how students use that same equipment to investigate the impact of heat on a range of physical and chemical reactions.

During the pre-observation conference, coaches may find that many novice bilingual and dual-language teachers need a great deal of support in matching what the program is with how they use practices to ensure student success in the classroom. Knowing the right practices to match with the program's unique bilingual and dual-language model will improve coaches' ability to help teachers as they plan new practices that they may have found from a wide range of bilingual and dual-language models.

During the pre-observation conference, not only will coaches need to listen for instructional strategies that are part of the lesson design, they'll also want to discuss how teachers leverage language as an instructional tool within the lesson, including which languages will be used and for what purpose. They should also discuss language as a factor in grouping strategies, and whether or not students should ever use one language as a means to learn the other during the same lesson. Each bilingual and dual-language program model has its own filter to keep out practices that don't match.

Figure 5.5 offers guiding questions to ensure program alignment.

Guiding Questions	How does this lesson reflect the program model?
	What aspects of the lesson do not reflect the program model?
	What other strategies or researched-based methods would you like to learn more about that could improve this lesson?
	What strategies will you implement to meet the range of literacy levels, content learning, and language proficiencies? Should these strategies use multiple languages and incorporate neglected strengths of students, cultural backgrounds, and so on?
Look-fors	
Reflections	

Figure 5.5: Guiding questions, look-fors, and reflections to ensure program alignment.

*Visit **go.SolutionTree.com/EL** for a free reproducible version of this figure.*

Check in With a Specialist

This last step should happen, as needed, right after the pre-observation conference. Once coaches have concluded the pre-observation conference with the teacher, they'll want to immediately take a few moments to jot down their reflections for any pertinent guiding questions. A critical part of this reflection process is identifying any practices, methods, or other areas of the lesson discussed that the coach may not understand or be familiar with, and that require the expert explanation that specialists are able to provide.

In your school or district, a specialist might be a district bilingual or dual-language coordinator, an ESL specialist, or anyone at the building or district level who has unique knowledge and training in serving the needs of this particular student population. Almost every district has one.

The final set of guiding questions can also help coaches find the right words to accurately ask language specialists about any uncertainties that the coach may still have. At times these check-ins with specialists will be more like lifelines for coaches who are still new to these classrooms. More often than not, these check-ins simply offer coaches the context and background knowledge necessary to accurately observe and provide feedback on a lesson's design, delivery, and outcome. When coaches are willing to consult those who have specialized training and expertise in a particular bilingual and dual-language model, it is a testament to their dedication to a coaching cycle that ensures fairness, equity, and focus on student learning.

Finally, coaches might also find that they need another perspective for vetting an idea or recommendation they want to ensure is in line with the program. Effective coaches use a range of coordinators, dual-language directors, bilingual lead teachers, and others to talk through their thought processes.

One cautionary note: coaches who don't speak the language of instruction must resist the urge to use these check-ins to ask specialists who are bilingual to translate lessons for them. This practice does not help coaches to be effective in the observation and feedback cycle. Asking for translations forces specialists to divert many hours to a task that helps only that coach—hours they should use toward tasks and activities that help students. Translating lesson plans also creates a false sense of knowing exactly what is going to be said and done during the lesson, when the reality is that translations are never exact in meaning and tone.

Translations from Spanish, with its many variations and dialects, are especially prone to inaccuracies in words and phrases. Furthermore, coaches who begin a habit of having others translate lessons for them face a high likelihood of disappointment when the growth of the bilingual and dual-language program prevents specialists from continuing to translate. Rather than placing the burden of translating lesson after lesson on the shoulders of specialists, coaches and bilingual and dual-language teachers are much better served by improving the way coaches use questions during the pre-observation conference to analyze the instructional design process.

Figure 5.6 (page 68) offers guiding questions to support check-ins with specialists.

Guiding Questions	What are some of the strategies the specialist champions that I wouldn't see in other classrooms? What additional data did you consider in planning and monitoring students' learning during the lesson? What additional resources, tools, and supplements do you plan to use? Is there anything you'd like for me to know for greater context before observing?
Look-fors	
Reflections	

Figure 5.6: Guiding questions, look-fors, and reflections for check-ins with specialists.

*Visit **go.SolutionTree.com/EL** for a free reproducible version of this figure.*

Conclusion

When I first started coaching teachers, the never-ending to-dos on my list of responsibilities often made me rush the first critical step in the pre-observation conference, which is to frame the foundation for teachers in order to ensure full transparency and buy-in. Teachers will appreciate coaches addressing these considerations and clarifiers to prepare for the complex nuances of bilingual and dual-language classrooms. This transparency and attention are key for coaches to leverage as they move into the actual observation, outlined in the next chapter.

Coaches can use the "Action-Planning Template" reproducible to help organize the learning from this chapter into smaller, more easily accomplished goals.

Chapter 5: Action-Planning Template

Use this chart to help you organize the learning from this chapter into smaller, more easily accomplished goals.

Next Steps	Time Line	Resources
1.		
2.		
3.		
4.		
5.		
6.		
7.		
8.		
9.		

The Observation

I must admit, when I began my journey as a consultant, I assumed that the same methods and tools I'd acquired through a monolingual context would help me coach teachers into greatness. Yet, when I went into classrooms where students spoke Urdu, Mandarin, Somali, or French, I knew that I could not use the same scripting process I learned during my days as an administrator. It's not that I didn't want to. Scripting was a practice that I had become incredibly effective at using and found very helpful in retracing the steps of the lesson. However, when the language of instruction exceeded my mere bilingualism (Spanish and English), I quickly accepted that there was no way to utilize a business-as-usual approach.

Let's imagine that I entered a French immersion classroom with the goal of trying to observe the sequence and taxonomy of questioning as part of the school's larger focus. A number of things might have happened. First, I would have tried to script the questions using the disconnected pieces of sounds and language that I was able to comprehend. Second, I would have approximated and projected those sounds into the nearest word or concept in my schema as a part of my natural human need to make meaning and find patterns. Third, in the struggle to make meaning of so much inaccessible language, I might have allowed my joy of losing myself in the beauty of a new language to get the best of me and succumbed to my bias toward and fascination I feel for the French culture and language—and all languages, to be honest. However, each of these three outcomes would have decreased the teacher's trust in my ability to coach and impeded my ability to provide the kind of feedback that leads to improved outcomes for students.

There is no getting around the impossibility of scripting a lesson in a language the coach does not speak. Accepting this rather than moving forward with the rest of the monolingual framework can be liberating. It opens the door for coaches to adopt a more effective, but parallel, process that minimizes the potential of error by observers and increases the effectiveness of next steps for teachers (Pianta & Hamre, 2009). In other words, by releasing our need to fit a square peg into a round hole, we actually recreate the conditions to improve outcomes for bilingual and dual-language students.

When coaches enter a bilingual and dual-language classroom to begin their observations, they should not expect to find a specific sequence to how learning in these very complex spaces happens. Effective bilingual and dual-language classrooms are dynamic environments in which it may be necessary to veer from the daily schedule in order to match evidence-based practices more effectively with the needs of students to ensure that every student meets the objectives of the lesson being observed. In addition to the number of course corrections that teachers make while delivering instruction, the complexity of observing these classrooms when a coach doesn't understand the language requires coaches to be disciplined in their observation methods. Through this discipline, coaches are able to accurately observe and provide powerful feedback. The starting place for this method is identifying the most essential questions to be closely investigated and answered as a result of the coach's observation.

The essential questions serve as a guide that helps the coach focus on the key interactions, observe and analyze students' responses, gather additional evidence and information, revise thinking in order to improve accuracy relative to the essential question, and move on to the next essential question to continue the process. Using these questions to guide the observation is imperative to ensuring that coaches observe all elements of classroom instruction and have the information they need to provide effective feedback.

Four Essential Questions for Guiding Observations

Observing bilingual and dual-language teachers begins with reviewing the four essential questions. These questions provide the necessary context that coaches miss when they do not understand the language. The four essential questions are as follows.

1. Are safety, equity, and agency present for all students so they can access learning?
2. Is there a community of respect that maximizes instructional time and focus?
3. Does the instructional design help students master rigorous content, acquire more complex academic language, think critically about relevant uses, and build independence?
4. Are the practices, skills, and strategies observed accurately implemented and aligned to the program's vision and goals?

These four essential questions act as guideposts that steer the coach's path of inquiry. They are like lenses to help coaches focus, since they cannot pull that information from other interactions grounded in language. Most important, these questions help coaches immediately prioritize what they observe and how it shapes the feedback teachers need to improve their practice. This process differs greatly from traditional observation methods in most general education settings where the coach understands the language of instruction. In these cases, coaches are expected to script the lesson during the observation and then analyze that transcription later. While this observation method is intended to increase accuracy, it assumes three things: (1) coaches can transcribe everything said and done by the twenty or thirty people involved in a lesson; (2) coaches' transcriptions are a factual and objective record of what took place, and this record is void of error, as though it were recorded by a machine; and (3) coaches analyzing this record against an evaluation framework that defines good teaching is the most efficient and accurate way to improve teacher practice.

Monolingual coaches, especially, should give themselves license to analyze the interactions and information they observe to improve the accuracy of their conclusions.

Are Safety, Equity, and Agency Present for All Students so They Can Access Learning?

The essential questions signal how much information coaches need to accurately provide high-leverage feedback. For example, the first question asks coaches to observe and collect evidence around aspects of safety, equity, and agency. We cannot expect students to do their best learning if they feel unsafe, like second-class citizens, or powerless over any aspect of their own education journey. For bilingual and dual-language students, challenges in safety, equity, and agency raise a student's affective filter. This affective filter serves as a shield that protects students from potential harm by filtering or limiting language in or out. Students who shut down their ability to interact with language can't master the content, can't produce language, and can't access the social network of schools that allows them to meaningfully interact with others. That is why it's important to prioritize collecting these data among the range of feedback that improves teacher practice and outcomes for bilingual and dual-language students.

The first essential question asks observers to analyze whether there is substantial evidence that the safety, equity, and agency necessary for students to learn content and language are in place. In other words, is every student physically and emotionally safe? Does the teacher value students' identities and contributions as invaluable members of the learning community? Bilingual and dual-language classrooms reflect diverse languages, dialects, social classes, races, beliefs about family, notions about school, hygiene habits, approaches to conflict resolution, and views on identity. This list, as long as it already is, only represents a fraction of the many facets of culture and identity that define these students.

No educator would want to raise a hand in a crowded room and broadcast that he or she doesn't believe all students can learn. Nor would an educator want to volunteer that deep down inside, he or she believes some students and families shouldn't have the right to do what they feel is best for themselves. But hints of these beliefs come out in the classroom in both subtle and less subtle ways, hence the need to start thinking about feedback through the lens of the first essential question.

For example, a teacher might not like students visiting loved ones in another country two weeks before winter break. Is it a problem because these students are missing school, or is it a manifestation of a culture that puts family above all else? Or, a teacher might tell students that specific phrases or words are not real Spanish because he or she speaks a different dialect. Is it a problem that some students know the word *perrito*, *jocho*, or *pancho* for *hot dog*, or is it an opportunity to explore the richness and diversity of language? More importantly, do we look at language learners and see a laundry list of things they can't do and don't know, or do we see all the amazing things they can do and do know? The shift is subtle, but it can change how welcomed and valued students feel.

Confronting negative mindsets is one of the most challenging conversations a coach can have with a teacher. Author and Harvard Business School professor emeritus John P. Kotter (2012) shares that significant change must begin by "identifying and discussing crises, potential crises, or major opportunities" (p. 21). I couldn't agree with Kotter more. The mismatch in our beliefs about what bilingual and dual-language students can do and the reality of what they are capable of if provided the right tools and supports is a potential crisis that effective coaching can transform into a major opportunity. Changing this mismatch must precede all other considerations if teachers who serve bilingual and dual-language students are to improve student outcomes.

Coaches who note challenges related to safety, equity, and agency during the observation should continue observing and collecting evidence of strengths and opportunities for growth. However, they are already gathering the most important feedback that can help teachers improve student outcomes. By continuing the observation, coaches can gain important insight into what is happening and why it is taking place. In other words, coaches might observe that students didn't meet the objective of the lesson (the what). However, the coach can trace the reason students didn't meet the objective back to issues of safety that raised their affective filter (the why). In the end, identifying patterns of practice increases the coach's accuracy and feedback.

Is There a Community of Respect That Maximizes Instructional Time and Focus?

The second essential question asks coaches to observe and collect evidence regarding whether there is a community of respect in the classroom that maximizes students' time and ability to focus on learning. Bilingual and dual-language teachers must double what monolingual students learn in general education classrooms—language learners need to master the content standards as well as the academic language necessary to access those standards. In order to accomplish this, teachers must have efficient procedures, routines, and organizational structures that help them focus their time on learning rather than managing behaviors and lagging transitions.

For example, even in monolingual classrooms, it's normal to walk into a classroom where there are many different definitions of how to give and show respect. These differences reflect the various cultural norms of the students in that classroom. For bilingual and dual-language teachers, building a community of respect that maximizes time is even more important because of the additional standards and areas that must be taught. Coaches must include time to observe and provide feedback about the identities, cultural norms, and values of each student as the basis for a classroom community of respect. This is an essential part of the coaching process, which is unique to these classrooms. Otherwise, teachers will struggle to engage students in the safe language and cognitive risk taking that are the lifeline of these classrooms.

Does the Instructional Design Help Students Master Rigorous Content, Acquire More Complex Academic Language, Think Critically About Relevant Uses, and Build Independence?

The third question asks coaches to consider if the observed lesson met its most important goal: helping bilingual and dual-language students master grade-level content while becoming proficient enough in the language of instruction to use this learning in their lives outside of school. This third essential question must be preceded, out of necessity, by the fundamental prerequisites of student safety and the time and focus needed for students to learn. While this essential question comes third, however, coaches should know that it should stand boldly at the heart of all educational systems.

After patterns of safety, time, and focus, what coaches observe as part of this third essential question provides some the most powerful feedback to improve teacher practice and student learning. More than any other, the question of effective instructional design cuts to the core of teaching and learning, even when coaches don't understand the language of instruction.

There are many effective instructional practices and strategies. However, even when implemented accurately, not all are effective or appropriate for the goals that inform the various programs that serve bilingual and dual-language students. By suspending their expectations of practices that don't align to program goals and preferences, coaches can motivate people to take action in the right direction. There's more buy-in for taking action when teachers feel a sense of shared responsibility and ownership over a common agenda.

Are the Practices, Skills, and Strategies Observed Accurately Implemented and Aligned to the Program's Vision and Goals?

Finally, the fourth essential question asks coaches to observe and collect evidence of practices, skills, and strategies for accurate implementation and alignment to the program's vision and goals. What makes this essential question so critical is that what defines good teaching in bilingual and dual-language classrooms is often different from their monolingual counterparts. Not only that, but what defines appropriate and good also depends on the program and the body of research that informs it. In a pull-out class of English as a second language (ESL or ELD) class, a coach is not likely to see the teacher fully deliver a lesson in Hmong. Rather, the coach would be more likely to see a highly scaffolded lesson delivered in English in which students use Hmong to make meaning and fill in the information they have yet to learn to articulate in English.

Conversely, in a third-grade, two-way dual-language classroom, one might see a strategy called *así se dice* (Escamilla et al., 2013). This strategy asks students to translate (or more accurately, transcreate, since exact translations are almost an impossibility due to the nuances of every language) a short text from one language to the other program language to explore the nuances of each language and the gaps in being able to express oneself with full ease and precision. While the teacher who uses this strategy might see its powerful impact on students developing their bilingualism and biliteracy, students who frequently engage in this strategy during an ESL lesson may not develop proficiency as quickly in English, since bilingualism is not the vision for ESL students. The focus of that translation has everything to do with how effective that strategy will be. That is why this question asks coaches to look at both the appropriateness of a strategy or practice for the program and the accuracy of implementation to ensure its effectiveness.

When coaches are observing and analyzing interactions in a language they don't speak, we can't count on the clarity of evidence from just those interactions. The essential questions help coaches gauge the effectiveness of interactions based on more structured criteria and purpose. Observing bilingual and dual-language teachers in this way reduces uncertainty and minimizes the assumptions that cloud accuracy.

Likewise, feedback must honestly explore teachers' mindsets about the language learner program model in which they teach. These program models can provoke heated debate because they tap into deeply held personal beliefs. Some programs guide educators to only use the LOTE in the early years before gradually transitioning into a balance of the LOTE and English instruction. Some programs guide teachers to begin in the LOTE before gradually transitioning students solely into English. Some balance the LOTE and English from day one, English and the LOTE for certain instructional purposes, and the two together in order to analyze and maximize what each student truly knows.

Teachers whose practices depart from the program model need honest and compassionate guidance to understand how their perceptions and differing practices might compromise a program designed to ensure student success. Often, these perceptions are a result of their lived language and learning journeys. I've met many brilliant and well-intentioned bilingual teachers who use an English-only approach behind closed doors because of the personal pain they felt when they were bullied or picked on for not speaking English or speaking it with an accent. Using these English-only approaches is not recommended because they prioritize personal feelings over research-based methods that we know are effective for bilingual and dual-language students.

In moments like these, the essential questions can point the coach toward constructive changes to improve teacher practice. However, the essential questions cannot be used alone as they require more substance. In addition to the essential questions, coaches need a more systematic way of collecting bias-free evidence about the impact of teachers' decisions and practice on the quality of student learning. The systematic close observation and evidence collection come from the six tasks of notice.

Six Tasks of Notice as Tools for Collecting Evidence

The *six tasks of notice* are a method I've devised for coaches to document what's occurred during an observation, especially when observing a lesson delivered in a language that the coach does not fully know. For many coaches, this process is generally known as collecting evidence. The exercises that comprise these six tasks of notice, which I refer to as *noticings*, decrease the strain of observing in another language. I designed them to help coaches employ a more responsible and honest approach than relying on intuition or simply "knowing" when good instruction is happening. Instead, these noticings train coaches to pay careful attention and accurately detect the effectiveness of teacher practices or actions and the more complex relationship among planning, instructional delivery, instructional adjustments, and student success.

Coaches should understand the following about the six tasks of notice.

- **They do not involve scripting:** Since coaches may not speak the language of the classroom, scripting requires too much guesswork. Instead of grounding observations and feedback in a script that relies on more guesses than certainties, coaches anchor observation and feedback cycles using four essential questions and six tasks of notice. They are structured to guide the process to a constructive path of improvement focused on students' individualized and program goals. By collaborating on the interpretation of each task of notice, coaches can provide more accurate and helpful steps than any broken script ever could.

- **They are aligned to all major teacher evaluation frameworks but designed to move beyond those frameworks to help coaches understand complex issues of culture, identity, and language that affect student learning outcomes:** Careful attention to the six tasks of notice can help a coach accurately detect evidence of inequities in the classroom. While this knowledge may lead to uncomfortable conversations with the teacher being observed, coaches must trust that evidence and begin the process of coaching with that evidence rather than fall back on another component in other teacher evaluation frameworks.

- **Teachers should use them together with the essential questions:** The six tasks of notice help coaches with the structured attention and accurate detection needed while observing bilingual and dual-language classrooms. However, coaches also need to analyze the evidence collected through these six tasks of notice. This analysis of evidence, together with the essential questions, will help coaches focus on what needs to improve. The six tasks of notice and the essential questions serve as two complementary components of the observation and feedback cycle. Their interrelationship increases the likelihood that the changes recommended by the coach will lead to improved outcomes for students. Only through this approach will coaching feedback maintain a parallel focus on real-time student learning and long-term program effectiveness.

Table 6.1 provides coaches with an overview of the four essential questions and six tasks of notice.

Table 6.1: Four Essential Questions and Six Tasks of Notice

Four Essential Questions	Six Tasks of Notice
1. Are safety, equity, and agency present for all students so they can access learning? 2. Is there a community of respect that maximizes instructional time and focus? 3. Is the instructional design effective in helping students master rigorous content, acquire more complex academic language, think critically about relevant uses, and build independence? 4. Are the practices, skills, and strategies observed accurately implemented and aligned to the program's vision and goals?	1. Environment and organization 2. Teacher-student interactions 3. Instructional strategies (practice, program, and content) 4. Cause-and-effect relationships 5. Learning tasks 6. Student agency over learning

Visit **go.SolutionTree.com/EL** *for a free reproducible version of this table.*

Coaches will need to learn the skill of *quieting*, or being fully present in the moment, to counter their mind's need to try to make meaning of and search for knowable chunks in what the teacher is saying. For monolingual coaches as well as those who know "just enough" of the language used in the lesson, an overestimation of the language they think they understand is the greatest threat to a fair process. By turning off the volume of what the teacher is saying, coaches can actively immerse themselves in observing the lesson and its ability to help students maximize learning and build independence. These six tasks help coaches focus on what students are learning instead of what the teacher is saying.

Using the same systems and tools for observation as in monolingual classrooms will likely create frustration, inconsistencies, and subjectivity. I designed the noticings to ensure that every observation and interaction have a purpose, a goal, and a strategic intentionality to ensure improved outcomes for students. Through ongoing practice with these tools, coaches build their capacity to collect evidence that is accurate, specific, objective, and based on context.

The six tasks of notice in table 6.2 (page 80) give coaches a more predictable and standardized way of noticing the effectiveness of bilingual and dual-language teacher practice on student learning and program success. Each task of notice consists of noticings—things the coach should be paying attention to. The standardized processes in the six tasks of notice work to simplify the complexity of bilingual and dual-language environments so coaches can improve the reliability of their interpretations, one task at a time, and increase the likelihood that their feedback leads to growth.

Table 6.2: Six Tasks of Notice and Noticings

Six Tasks of Notice	Noticings
1. Environment and organization	1. The quantity, quality, and authenticity of the print, language, and literacy environment 2. Routines and procedures 3. Respectful and student-centered classroom management 4. Beliefs and expectations
2. Teacher-student interactions	1. Affective interactions 2. Instructional interactions 3. Language interactions 4. Feedback interactions
3. Instructional strategies (practice, program, and content)	1. Pedagogical practices aligned to the program and implemented accurately 2. A variety of strategies, tools, and interactions for both content and language instruction
4. Cause-and-effect relationships	1. What the teacher is saying, doing, and showing 2. Students' responses, actions, questions, applications, and levels of dependence versus independence as a result of the teacher's actions
5. Learning tasks	1. Access to essential and rigorous grade-level content 2. Equal access to receptive and productive language supports that allow students to do and show their best learning 3. Integrated practice that is authentic to the diverse cultures and countries that speak the language of instruction and connects to students' diverse cultures and reference points
6. Student agency over learning	1. What students are learning 2. How students learned 3. What language goal students are working on

Visit go.SolutionTree.com/EL for a free reproducible version of this table.

While each task of notice provides critical insight into the effectiveness of instructional decisions, many will see that the following descriptions of three of the six tasks—teacher-student interactions, instructional strategies, and learning tasks—are much longer. This is not meant to elevate the importance of these tasks over others; however, these three areas seem to be more difficult for coaches to notice accurately. Bilingual and dual-language teachers spend more time explaining and helping coaches understand those tasks because they are the hardest to get right when they don't fully know the language of instruction.

Environment and Organization

The four noticings for this task of notice include:

1. The quantity, quality, and authenticity of the print, language, and literacy environment
2. Routines and procedures

3. Respectful and student-centered classroom management
4. Beliefs and expectations

The first task of notice asks coaches to notice the environment and organization of the classroom. This is the most transparent of all the tasks of notice, and coaches can complete this task in a matter of minutes. Additionally, because environment is a relatively fixed factor (for example, a classroom library that stays in place, giving coaches the time they need to notice its details), rather than changing (like a question the teacher asks), coaches find safety in noticing many aspects of quantity and authenticity in the print environment and evidence of the routines and procedures needed for efficiency and focus.

The environment plays a key role in bilingual and dual-language classrooms. It must function efficiently, helping students access the resources, materials, and tools they need to be successful. It must also clearly support the routines, procedures, and management systems that allow the teacher to maximize learning time. Finally, and most important, it must create a climate that is conducive for every learner to engage in his or her best learning.

The Quantity, Quality, and Authenticity of the Print, Language, and Literacy Environment

The first noticing under task of notice 1 is the quantity, quality, and authenticity of the print, language, and literacy environment. Grade-appropriate items in the classroom should be present in all languages used in the classroom. Word walls with equal prominence for all languages should have their own dedicated space. Read-alouds and anchor charts should reflect the language of instruction. There should be a classroom library for each program language and an abundance of language supports, like anchor charts and sentence stems. Authentic centers (or those that reflect the methods, practices, and texts of the culture represented in the language) in all languages can provide powerful tools for students to build independence, reinforce practice, and have a variety of opportunities to engage with language and literacy. For example, a coach might note all print resources organized by color (such as Spanish resources labeled in red and English resources labeled in blue).

Another aspect to note is whether these print, language, and literacy resources across program languages offer equal representation, use, and access for all learners who need them. While it may seem obvious, coaches should also remark on any furniture, spaces, or materials that might pose a safety risk to students. Finally, coaches should be able to spot a functional space for each instructional strategy used throughout the day, including whole group, small group, partners, and independent work, with language, content, and contextualized supports readily available for successful participation and learning.

Routines and Procedures

The second noticing task of notice 1 is the effectiveness of the routines and procedures that allow the teacher to maximize instructional time. Routines and procedures can make or break the flow of a lesson. When effective systems are in place, students are able to cofacilitate the signals, procedures, and structures to move from one learning chunk to another, and from one place in the room to the next. Even kindergarteners are capable of learning that when the music begins to play, it means that they should begin cleaning up their area or go to the rug.

Respectful and Student-Centered Classroom Management

The next and most challenging component of the environment is maintaining a respectful and student-centered classroom management system. This system must include prevention, awareness, reinforcement, and response to both positive and negative student behaviors. The question is whether these rules serve the adults only or honor and build from students' cultural, social, and academic needs. For example, are there harsh consequences for students who talk in class because the teacher prefers a quiet learning environment, even though students can effectively attend to learning while interacting with peers (which also supports their language goals)? This is an example of serving the adults versus serving the students.

When teachers take student backgrounds and perspectives into account, success is easier to achieve. It also helps to communicate to students that every class member should respect the learning environment because it was created by and for everyone—not just the teacher. This doesn't imply that negative behaviors won't ever take place. There will likely be some students during the course of the year who do not follow the most collaboratively designed behavior management system. During those times, coaches should be willing to note the behavior, observe the teacher response, and find the causal relationship between what the student did, what the teacher did, and whether the learning environment was preserved for every student.

Beliefs and Expectations

The noticing at the core of this task is how well the coach is able to perceive and accurately interpret the teachers' high expectations and belief that every learner is capable, intelligent, and worthy of high levels of academic, linguistic, and social achievement. Coaches will most likely not be able to note a set of beliefs, especially when they don't speak the language used in the classroom. However, even in a language they don't understand, coaches can observe equity in expectations, procedures, and respect in the efficiency and student ownership of procedures.

The use of culturally relevant signals to facilitate transitions, such as a short French song typically sung in Quebec to signal the time allotted for moving from one task to the next, can also be very telling. Coaches can observe a variety of means to communicate expectations to students, like the use of task cards and oral review, even while teachers instruct in a language that the coach doesn't fully understand. The goal of these routines, procedures, and management strategies is to establish the optimal environment and circumstances for students to focus on rigorous and meaningful learning that leads to independent application of that learning beyond the walls of the school.

High expectations for student participation and learning are also necessary, as long as those expectations are realistic and appropriate to each student's stage of language development. Teachers must plan and coaches must support this line between high expectations and realistic expectations for every student, including those new to the country or just new to that particular language.

Teacher-Student Interactions

The four noticings for this task of notice include:

1. Affective interactions
2. Instructional interactions
3. Language interactions
4. Feedback interactions

The second task of notice is a natural extension of the first. Coaches go from observing and collecting evidence about the effectiveness of the environment and conditions for learning to collecting evidence of the countless interactions that take place between teachers and students and among students themselves. It provides critical information for responding to the first essential question: Are safety, equity, and agency present for all students so they can access learning?

These four noticings give monolingual coaches a concentrated glimpse inside each encounter, interaction, and response—even without understanding the exact words used during those interactions. In part, the evidence coaches collect during this task provides that glimpse by moving beyond just identifying the quantity of exchanges to actually examining the quality, purpose, and equity of each encounter. When teachers align the trend data they gather from these noticings to the essential questions, they highlight interactional patterns that coaches can use to identify strengths and challenges with clarity. In general, there are three questions coaches should ask themselves as they observe these interactions: (1) What role does the teacher have? (2) What role do the students have? (3) Do these interactions work in service of all learners and support greater achievement?

Affective Interactions

The first noticing focuses on interactions that influence students' affective filters. It asks the coach to collect evidence of interactions that foster and reinforce relationships, acknowledge students' feelings and contributions, and lower anxiety. Coaches collect these data by naming, categorizing, and tallying the range of encounters. They might ask themselves, "Do individuals treat each other in kind, welcoming, and caring ways in the classroom?" or "Do all or just some students experience that same warmth?" Coaches can develop a pretty accurate picture of these affective encounters by noting the many personal interactions that take place during a lesson and the ways that the interactions between teachers and students strengthen relationships and increase academic and linguistic risk taking. Further, coaches should notice whether they see a balanced pattern of these affective interactions across different genders, language levels, locations in the room, or some other relevant factor.

Figure 6.1 offers a generic template for tallying affective interactions, or those exchanges throughout the lesson that influence the relationships and the emotional connections students forge with the teacher, their peers, and their learning environment. The template includes columns for exchanges that have a positive or negative impact, including general exchanges (like telling a student, "Great job!") and specific exchanges (like a teacher telling a student, "Look at this! I see that you practiced your writing goal here using some compound sentences, and you even highlighted where you added them. I know this was a hard goal, but aren't you so proud of how it improved the way your story reads?").

The first column lists a number of affective considerations that are observable without access to the language, with space for coaches to add additional strategies or practices. The second column asks coaches to identify who is interacting with the student: is it a teacher-student interaction (T-S) or student-student interaction (S-S)?

The next two sets of columns ask coaches to tally the number of interactions that fit within each look-for and whether they are general or specific. For example, if the teacher uses eye contact and smiles at the class, the coach places a tally mark in the positive (general) column. If the teacher encourages an individual student, the coach tallies that interaction in the positive (specific) column. On the other hand, if the coach observes the teacher correcting the language that a specific student or group of students produces, he or she would tally it under one of the last two

Affective Look-fors	Teacher (T-S) Student (S-S)	Positive (General)	Positive (Specific)	Negative (General)	Negative (Specific)
Recognition of students' assets					
Sensitivity for student identity					
Encouragement of academic risks					
Behaviors like eye contact, smiles, and laughter					
Correction of language production					

Figure 6.1: Tallying affective interactions.

*Visit **go.SolutionTree.com/EL** for a free reproducible version of this figure.*

negative columns because of its potential to lower the affective filter. Just as with the positive columns, the negatives can be marked as *general* or *specific*.

This template is a useful tool for coaches who want a closer and more objective look at how well classroom interactions foster the affect, or emotions, necessary for student success. Affect is essential in bilingual and dual-language classrooms. As Krashen (1987) notes, educators can lessen student anxiety with comprehensible input—a level of language that they are able to understand and most effectively built on content that students are interested in hearing. According to Krashen (1987), "These methods do not force early production in the second language, but allow students to produce when they are 'ready,' recognizing that improvement comes . . . not from forcing and correcting production" (pp. 6–7). In other words, even well-meaning interactions can lower self-confidence and increase anxiety levels, which create powerful mental blocks that impede learning.

Instructional Interactions

The second noticing focuses on instructional interactions, which are interactions grounded in the content objectives for the day rather than the cultural or social language interactions of a classroom. When coaches notice instructional interactions, the issue of who is doing the work and what work they are doing is paramount. What are teachers doing? How do they make students aware of the goal of instruction? Do they provide a range of activities designed to get students interacting with new content that builds from what they already know? In the end, these interactions should be authentic, meaningful, and highly contextualized according to students' schema so students are able to integrate new information from the lesson rather than overcome challenges presented by a mismatch in background knowledge. Moreover, the range of instructional interactions should provide access to and support for the two sets of standards that all bilingual and dual-language learners must master: grade-level content standards and language development standards.

Language Interactions

The third noticing focuses on language interactions, or how teachers use, elevate, and differentiate academic language in the classroom. In a classroom that serves language learners, this is one of the leading differentiators from other classrooms. But here is the conundrum: coaches must sometimes note how students use language when they themselves don't speak the language. How can a monolingual coach accurately do this in a bilingual and dual-language setting? Admittedly, observing instruction in another language has its fair share of challenges. Coaches can, however, take some practical steps to efficiently document how teachers intentionally develop and support language to promote continuous and uninterrupted growth. Four practices in particular can help coaches who don't speak the language of instruction still objectively observe in any bilingual and dual-language classroom: (1) scaffolding and supplementary materials and resources that match language proficiency, (2) teacher changes in language, (3) student changes in language, and (4) alignment of language tools.

The first practice to note is teachers' intentionality in how they scaffold language to ensure growth for all learners. Remember that scaffolds are temporary structures that help students access or use a new language. Like the scaffolding of a building, once the structure is secure, that scaffold is removed and the next language goal is set. Students just beginning language acquisition might go through a silent period and require a great many visual supports to connect language and texts to their meaning. But not all learners need that. Students who are further along in their journey may require greater opportunities to explore how they can use their two languages and correctly apply new vocabulary, grammar, and sentence structure.

For a variety of reasons, however, such as limited formative assessment of language development or misunderstanding of the typical taxonomy of language skills, time, and ease, not all bilingual and dual-language classrooms approach scaffolds in such an intentional way. The idea that some learners may need a scaffold that others do not might seem strange. Many teachers have told me that this was an option they had never even considered. That is why it deserves a coach's thoughtful consideration.

Feedback Interactions

The fourth and final noticing is to observe and record evidence of feedback from the teacher to the student either through interactions or in print. Feedback is one of the primary ways to guide students to improve both their content learning and language growth. As such, the qualities of effective feedback outlined in table 6.3 only scratch the surface. Nevertheless, they should help coaches identify evidence of effective and ineffective use of feedback.

Table 6.3: Qualities of Effective Feedback in Bilingual and Dual-Language Classrooms

Content Feedback	Language Feedback
• Celebrates and names academic risks • Celebrates or guides deep thinking • Provides direction to correct major misconceptions • Times feedback well so students have an opportunity to incorporate feedback into mastery of content goals • Demonstrates equity in the amount and frequency of feedback each student receives • Listens to students actively and accurately addresses the source of any misunderstandings	• Follows a formula of comprehensible input + the language use of just one level higher than the student's current proficiency level + meaningful opportunities to practice new language in a variety of ways • Celebrates and names linguistic risks • Provides direction that first ensures comprehension and then integration of new language goals • Celebrates or guides cross-linguistic connections (students' awareness of the language choices they make so they are more intentional) • Demonstrates sensitivity and care for the relationship and cultural norms of interactions between teachers and students and across genders • Delivers feedback through a collaborative dialogue using the four domains of listening, speaking, reading, and writing

*Visit **go.SolutionTree.com/EL** for a free reproducible version of this table.*

Instructional Strategies (Practice, Program, and Content)

The two noticings for this task of notice include:

1. Pedagogical practices aligned to the program and implemented accurately
2. A variety of strategies, tools, and interactions for both content and language instruction

This task of notice is rooted in the different programs that serve bilingual and dual-language learners, building initiatives, and other key school-based contexts. Monolingual coaches who observe in bilingual and dual-language classrooms will see that building background knowledge and expertise improves their ability to recognize instructional strategies. This background knowledge in second language acquisition and best practice provides the foundation coaches need to skillfully analyze the decisions that teachers make regarding practices and strategies in the lesson. However, some coaches will find that they still don't have the solid footing in language acquisition theories and program features necessary to determine things like accuracy, alignment, and explicitness in another language.

Some school leaders have asked me why they should sequence this particular task of notice as third in the process if programs are constantly striving toward an end goal of student achievement and program coherence. In short, through these two noticings, coaches are able to answer the final essential question: Are the practices, skills, and strategies observed accurately implemented and aligned to the program's vision and goals? This question is the heart of this task of notice. And as the heart, these two noticings determine if and how coaches approach the remaining tasks.

Pedagogical Practices Aligned to the Program and Implemented Accurately

The first noticing embedded in the instructional strategies is that of making sure pedagogical practices align to the program and its implementation. During this first noticing, it is important for coaches to put aside the need or desire to understand the lesson. This is one of those pesky habits that monolingual coaches are used to doing, which causes them to misunderstand a lot of the language they think they understand and miss the real evidence. They should stop trying to determine whether they understand the words spoken in the classroom—it is not the point of the lesson nor the observation.

Instead, coaches should strive to recognize and name each of the processes that signal the range of verbal, interactive, learner, language, and literacy strategies and practices the teacher uses. Even though many coaches are unable to understand what teachers are saying and writing in the instructional strategies being observed, they can use this task of notice to detect the variety and accuracy of these instructional strategies. Coaches are also more than capable of being cognizant of the ways that tools provided by teachers give students opportunities to practice and apply those instructional strategies. Here is a sample of what a coach might note when observing a teacher's five procedural steps.

1. The teacher identifies three types of verbal interactions for use during class discussions.
2. The teacher discusses a range of content, language, and cultural learning goals with students and records them on a chalkboard or whiteboard at the front of the class, along with visual cues, for everyone to see.
3. The teacher displays sentence frames for students and holds one for them to see.
4. The teacher has students pair up for brief student-to-student conversations on the focus of the lesson.
5. The teacher smiles and provides feedback that is well received by students.

This outline of procedural steps is all the coach needs to capture during the observation. There is no minimum or limit to the number of practices or strategies he or she observes. However, once the coach sees a transition, this usually indicates that the strategy has concluded. At some point after this, whether it is immediately after observing the practice or after leaving the classroom altogether, coaches must begin using those procedural steps to identify the strategy. A strategy is a method, whereas a procedure identifies the steps that the method entails. By understanding the steps in a strategy or method, coaches can backward-map what they are observing.

Some novice coaches struggle to connect visible features with their respective practices because there are so many possible practices to see in the sequence of behaviors and scaffolds they collect. In the midst of so much material, coaches might forget this task of notice altogether. However, this task is well worth the work. When I work with instructional leaders and coaches, I often suggest that coaches scaffold this task by using the pre-observation conference to first identify one key instructional strategy that will be used during the lesson. Then coaches can use that information to meticulously note what they can discern from each step in the strategy.

Figure 6.2 (page 90) provides a broad observational tool that can help coaches in collecting this type of data. In the first column, coaches write the observable steps teachers take in using various strategies. In the second column, they record any techniques or resources that ensure comprehensibility for all students during

Observation of Instructional Practices and Strategies		
Features and Procedural Steps of Research-Based Strategies	Tools for Ensuring Comprehensible Input	Structures and Resources to Support Student Independence

Figure 6.2: Observation of instructional practices and strategies.

*Visit **go.SolutionTree.com/EL** for a free reproducible version of this figure.*

the lesson, such as realia or some other visual supports. In the third column, they record structures and resources students receive that support their ability to apply what they learned independently, such as anchor charts or anything that communicates individual goals students should be working on. Coaches should also note those times when there are no opportunities for independent application of what students learned in the lesson.

A Variety of Strategies, Tools, and Interactions for Both Content and Language Instruction

Instead of focusing on just one instructional strategy, some coaches prefer to use this task of notice to collect data on the full range of instructional strategies used. Coaches then check in with specialists who are better trained to help correctly match the procedural steps observed with the corresponding instructional strategies. This ability to match procedural steps with the right strategy requires collaboration with someone who knows the program, its practices, and the need for confidentiality in sharing observational data of another teacher. Coaches can find specialists who can serve as collaborative resources in a variety of places.

The first potential candidate for collaboration is the teacher who was observed. This teacher knows better than anyone else the strategies, comprehensible input, and resources for student independence that they are working toward. Choosing the observed teacher for consultation also holds some hidden benefits like building shared investment and ownership in the process through transparency. This also provides the observed teacher with additional opportunities to reflect on how explicit and accurate his or her teaching moves were relative to the intended goals.

Choosing this collaboration also allows the teacher and coach to exchange roles, creating a powerful dynamic between the two parties that can serve as a catalyst for honest dialogue addressing areas of improvement. It's as if the coach were saying, "Look, I'm not perfect, and I want to learn from you." As a result, when it comes time for the teacher to expose his or her faults, a groundwork for the trust necessary to do so is already in place.

Equally helpful candidates for collaboration exist within and outside the building. District bilingual and dual-language instructional specialists, coordinators, and directors are wonderful resources to validate coaching observations. Coaches should keep open lines of communication with this team, particularly as coaches shift from observing to connecting observations to practices and strategies, and then to determining the accuracy and appropriate match of such practices and strategies to the program that classroom uses.

Bilingual and dual-language learners need access to instructional strategies and experiences that offer frequent and varied opportunities to interact with content, language, and culture. Teachers, in turn, need a range of instructional strategies to provide their students those opportunities. The repeated engagement with grade-level concepts and the language needed to access and discuss that content are essential elements for improving student achievement levels. The following questions can help coaches increase how accurately they interpret the evidence they have collected during this task of notice.

- Are teachers and students using and interacting with grade-level and rigorous content (the context of what students will learn) and the corresponding language (how students will receive and use language to learn it) needed to access that content (WIDA Consortium, 2010)?
- Do students get time to listen, speak, read, and write in meaningful ways and see how each of these language domains rely on each other (Gottlieb & Hamayan, 2007; Spolsky, 1989; Vygotsky, 1962)?
- Do students receive equal opportunities to interact with the content by having an accurate match between the instructional supports and their language proficiency (Gibbons, 2002, 2009; Gottlieb, Katz, & Ernst-Slavit, 2009; Vygotsky, 1962)? This ensures that scaffolds are provided when and to whom they are needed, and in the appropriate manner (Zwiers, O'Hara, & Pritchard, 2014).

The template in figure 6.3 (page 92) offers one way for coaches to capture the range and variety of strategies the teacher used. Tallying these instructional strategies, or others used to better meet the needs of students, gives a high-level

Student Name	Language Domain	Whole Group	Small Group	Paired Practice	Scaffolds	Discussion	Categories	Cross-Linguistic Connections	Learner Strategies

Range of strategies and interactions:
☐ Whole Group ☐ Small Group ☐ Partnered Practice ☐ Scaffolding Strategies ☐ Discussion Techniques
☐ Grouping ☐ Cross-Linguistic Connections ☐ Learner Strategies

Notes:

Figure 6.3: Observing the variety of strategies, tools, and interactions with content and language.

Visit go.SolutionTree.com/EL for a free reproducible version of this figure.

awareness of what strategies teachers are using, when they are using them, and whom these strategies are being used to support.

This template is a great tool for coaches to use to get an overview of the complexity and range of decisions bilingual and dual-language teachers must make. Coaches can use this tool by listing students' names in the first column and the initial of the language domain observed (R for reading, W for writing, S for speaking, or L for listening) in the second column, and placing a check in any of the next three columns (whole group, small group, paired practice). In the scaffolds column, coaches note whether teachers scaffolded the lesson and tasks accordingly. In the discussion column, coaches can identify whether students had the opportunity to talk about their learning. Under categories, coaches should identify the way that teachers formed categories for grouping, if this was observable. Coaches can use codes such as literacy level (LL), first language (L1), bilingual pairs (BP), or proficiency level (P) to record the categories. The last two columns give coaches a place to check off whether students were provided a means of applying their cross-linguistic connections or learner strategies. Finally, the bottom of the template provides additional space for coaches to recount or add more details, remarks, or notes to describe both teacher and student actions, as well as teacher and student responses to those actions.

Cause-and-Effect Relationships

The fourth task of notice serves as a complementary task to the previous data collection on instructional strategies. It is the first task of notice that truly asks coaches to draw conclusions about cause-and-effect relationships during their observation. It can also pose some challenges for coaches as they work to accurately and effectively identify cause-and-effect relationships as they occur.

However, I encourage coaches to push past this phase of productive struggle. The evidence that this task provides helps answer a four-part question: Was the learning design by teachers effective in helping students (1) master rigorous content, (2) acquire more complex academic language, (3) build on greater critical thinking skills, and (4) develop the ability to apply learning independently to other relevant contexts? Without the benefit of knowing the language, coaches must look to these markers as a guide. Two noticings embedded in cause-and-effect relationships provide supporting evidence about the practices that coaches observe during the cause-and-effect relationships task of notice.

1. What the teacher is saying, doing, and showing
2. Students' responses, actions, questions, applications, and levels of dependence versus independence as a result of the teacher's actions

Figure 6.4 provides a template coaches can use for collecting evidence of cause-and-effect relationships. This is just one example of a strategic tool coaches can use, depending on the nature of the relationship they are exploring. Coaches should choose the data collection tools that best meet the structure of the lesson and observation. This is especially important to note when lessons undergo changes from what the teacher originally planned. Coaches can use this template by simply noting what they observed the teacher doing, the resulting behavior or action from students, and any response (adjustments or reinforcements) that they observed after that.

Evidence of Cause-and-Effect Relationships		
Teacher (T)	Student (S)	Adaptations or Reinforcements
What was done . . . What was used . . . What was said . . .	Resulting action . . . Resulting resource used . . . Resulting questions . . .	What was done . . . What was used . . . What was said . . .
Interactions: ☐ Teacher-Student ☐ Student-Student ☐ Whole Group ☐ Small Group ☐ Individualized **Outcome of Input:** ☐ Independence ☐ Dependence		

Figure 6.4: Cause-and-effect observation template.

*Visit **go.SolutionTree.com/EL** for a free reproducible version of this figure.*

Since this task of notice requires coaches to combine evidence collection with drawing conclusions by matching cause-and-effect relationships, using the most effective template allows coaches to access the relationships that are most important to note. It also helps coaches to logically organize the factors involved since most coaches aren't fully bilingual, making scripting an unlikely option. Finally, as coaches gain confidence in their ability to match which teacher actions led to particular student results, they can either use the general template in figure 6.4 or choose not to use templates at all.

Regardless of the tools used, coaches should identify the following list of high-leverage cause-and-effect relationships. This list details a number of them that are fairly simple to spot, even in another language. They also represent indicators of effective planning and instructional delivery of the content objective, language development, and cultural connections vital to improving the achievement of language learners.

- Inclusion or exclusion of background knowledge
- Inclusion or exclusion of comprehensible input that matches students' needs
- Inclusion or exclusion of questioning techniques

- Inclusion or exclusion of varied presentations
- Inclusion or exclusion of clear directions
- Inclusion or exclusion of demonstrations or modeling
- Impact of moving instruction from the whole group into small groups
- Impact of moving instruction from small groups into partners or independent practice

In addition to students' immediate actions and responses, a good place to begin looking for evidence of cause-and-effect relationships is the range of tasks and varied assessments that serve as a time line of student learning. These assessments could include portfolios, learning logs, exit tickets, questions and discussions, student journals, projects, presentations, and additional student work samples not listed here.

Learning Tasks

The three noticings for this task of notice include the following.

1. Access to essential and rigorous grade-level content
2. Equal access to receptive and productive language supports that allow students to do and show their best learning
3. Integrated practice that is authentic to the diverse cultures and countries that speak the language of instruction and connects to students' diverse cultures and reference points

The fifth task of notice is a natural extension of the earlier ones, especially the first. Effective classroom environments are not the end goal, in and of themselves. We build effective classroom communities that create conditions for students to be successful. We intentionally interact with students and guide their interactions with each other to help them move closer to achieving their goals and beyond. All of these components merge when we look at learning tasks.

Coaches must look at the activities teachers give students with a unique and questioning lens, and a curiosity about what students are doing, why doing that activity matters, and how the activity might help students practice new learning in preparation for the real world. Coaches who support bilingual and dual-language classrooms will never be satisfied with observation worksheets that only offer isolated practices of pre-identified and decontextualized skills.

The three noticings of learning tasks occur together so coaches recognize the degree to which assigned tasks provide students ample practice and engagement with work they find worthy of their attention. They also aid coaches in recognizing learning tasks' alignment to the lesson goals, authenticity to students' cultures and the cultures of other speakers of this language worldwide, and appropriate scaffolding according to students' needs. However, the easiest way to collect evidence of learning tasks is to request a copy of learning activities from the teacher. Then coaches can use the following six questions to guide and facilitate a more collaborative conversation with the teacher.

1. Do learning tasks connect, align with, and incorporate content, language, and cultural goals?
2. Do learning tasks allow students to focus on making meaning?
3. Do learning tasks provide varied opportunities for when and how to apply new learning across goals?
4. Do learning tasks provide comprehensible input and scaffolds that give students a chance to process, produce, and reflect on their full linguistic abilities across all four domains?
5. Do learning tasks help students master the content through receptive (what students take in) and productive (what students produce) tasks that grow academic language?
6. Do learning tasks allow students to produce substantial written work daily? (Escamilla et al., 2013)

Student Agency Over Learning

The three noticings for this task include:

1. What students are learning
2. How students learned
3. What language goal students are working on

For coaches who don't speak the language of instruction, interacting with students to notice whether they have agency over what they are learning is the most accurate and effective way to shift real-time data collection from what students are taught to what they actually learn. Due to the nature of these interactions with language learners, however, coaches must approach this final task of notice with incredible sensitivity and caution. The prudence necessary to prepare for these interactions comes from the fact that it is the only time coaches interact directly with students during the observation. Nevertheless, coaches willing to abide by the following practices and recommendations will find that talking directly to students provides the best insight into their critical thinking and independent application of learning in the moment.

The coach confers with only one to three students at a time, and he or she should make every attempt to minimize interruptions to the learning process. Coaches preparing to directly observe students should be acutely aware of how even the quietest of interactions with students can disrupt the flow of learning, so they can make adjustments to the timing of those observations with students, when possible.

Coaches must remember the goal of these observations: to accurately collect a range of data that provide accurate insight into a teacher's decision-making process.

Coaches can use the following five practices to discover and promote student agency over learning.

1. **Keep quiet conversations with students to only one or two minutes:** Keeping a tight rein on the amount of time spent talking to students helps coaches maintain focus on student learning, which should always be the goal. This mindfulness also helps limit the amount of time students need to spend outside the target language, since it most likely happens in English. Finally, restricting the contact to two minutes or less and keeping the volume low enough for only two people to hear decrease the likelihood that other students will fixate and either build anxiety or excitement about whether the coach will put them on the spot next.

2. **Get a sense of who learners are before they enter the observation:** Coaches must consider questions such as, What are students' cultural backgrounds? What norms should they expect to see? What behaviors might be considered taboo or inappropriate? Educators have come to consider things like demanding eye contact and sitting in close proximity as essential actions to build a connection. However, when working with bilingual and dual-language classrooms, these actions might actually have the opposite effect. Coaches need to learn what is considered culturally appropriate for every student by learning about and gaining experiences in the cultures of the students served in that school community.

3. **Identify students' ability to interact in English if that is the only language the coach speaks:** Since these quick meetings normally happen in English, coaches need to know if a student has sufficient English skills for the conversation to be effective, or have access to another coach who is skilled at modifying the language of the conversation to match a student's English level. Either option requires understanding who the students are and an additional review of their data.

4. **Identify any students who are just beginning their language journey or are in their silent period:** Having a stranger put these students on the spot and ask them a series of questions can have some serious consequences on their feelings of safety, motivation to continue being a part of the classroom community, and confidence in their current language acquisition. It might benefit them to watch how these interactions work with their peers before asking them to take part in the process.

5. **Allow students to choose whether to accept an invitation to talk:** If coaches are looking for evidence of student agency, then students should have the power and authority to decline an interaction during the lesson. Some coaches can be overly pushy in trying to get students to answer their questions, while others might get offended and see this lack of response as an act of defiance or disrespect.

Since coaches review English and target language proficiency data during the pre-observation conference, they will have the language proficiency necessary to direct these brief meetings for any student selected. They should consider this prior knowledge essential context to ensure they inflict no harm while determining the degree of learning taking place. Following are the four most critical questions coaches should ask students during this meeting.

1. "What are you learning?" (This question provides insight into the activity's rigor, alignment, and student understanding of the lesson's content.)
2. "How did you learn that?" (This provides insight into students' metacognitive and problem-solving strategies.)
3. "Where else could you use these skills or strategies?" (This provides insight into whether students see the relevance and transferability of their new skills beyond the lesson or activity.)
4. "What language goal are you working on? How did you use it?" (This provides insight into comprehensible input, appropriateness of scaffolds, and integrated development of language alongside the content.)

Coaches shouldn't worry about the exact wording of these questions; rather, they should focus on the reassuring nature of the interaction and the intent of each question. They can rephrase questions, give examples, and so on, making them their own. This helps coaches maintain students' willingness to continue throughout the process and paint the most accurate picture of what students know and are able to do with that knowledge.

The questions and insights that manifest during these interactions are critical for coaches who spend most of their time in the classroom gathering evidence in another language. After being an administrator and working alongside coaches and administrators across the United States, I understand that these insights shine a light on answers to three questions that most educators want to know: (1) What do students know? (2) What are they able to do? and (3) Can they apply that learning when they need it most?

Conclusion

This chapter outlined strategies to help coaches mentally organize their observations in bilingual and dual-language classrooms using essential questions that point them to the most important ingredients for success during classroom observations. These essential questions combined with the tasks of notice provide a process that is far superior to scripting for coaches who are not fully proficient in the language of instruction. Having a clear process to collect accurate data without needing to rely on the actual words the teachers and students are using is key for a fair observation and feedback cycle. In the next chapter, we will look at the last crucial piece of the puzzle—the post-observation conference.

Coaches can use the "Action-Planning Template" reproducible (page 100) to help organize the learning from this chapter into smaller, more easily accomplished goals.

Chapter 6: Action-Planning Template

Use this chart to help you organize the learning from this chapter into smaller, more easily accomplished goals.

Next Steps	Time Line	Resources
1.		
2.		
3.		
4.		
5.		
6.		
7.		
8.		
9.		

The Post-Observation Conference

Coaches often ask themselves, "How can I provide fair feedback to bilingual and dual-language teachers? Is the documentation I created during each task of notice a valid starting point to recommend a series of actions that will improve student learning?" These are valid questions, but only if coaches have not received the training necessary to contribute to the success of bilingual and dual-language teachers. This chapter is the first step in receiving that critical training. It offers coaches insight into how to prioritize all the data collected during the observation so they can provide insight and feedback to the teacher for areas of improvement.

By now, coaches know the undeniable challenges posed by their inability to fully understand the language of instruction. However, these challenges need not disqualify coaches from coordinating honest and constructive teacher feedback with the necessary capacity-building efforts (or supports) that teachers need to implement feedback successfully. This coordination of feedback and support begins during the post-observation conference.

The post-observation conference is the fourth stage of the observation and feedback cycle. It helps coaches make the most of the mindset shifts that took place in stage 1 (see chapter 4, page 49) and what they learned in the pre-observation conference in stage 2 (see chapter 5, page 55). It further solidifies the context and insight into the teacher's thinking about the observed instructional strategies in stage 3 (see chapter 6, page 71). Regardless of whether the observation is announced or unannounced or formal or informal, the post-observation conference is key to providing the critical feedback that allows coaches and teachers to act on this feedback and measure the success of those efforts.

Preparation for the Post-Observation Conference

To best prepare for the post-observation conference, coaches will need to complete the following steps.

1. Share the data collected during the observation.
2. Clarify misconceptions that may exist in the coach's observations.
3. Identify trends of success regarding instructional planning, delivery, and assessment.
4. Consider multiple cause-and-effect relationships.
5. Verify earliest possible challenges to use as leverage points for the four essential questions.

Preparing for this very important conversation takes some planning. Coaches must carefully consider their approach in providing constructive criticism, support, and effective feedback to ensure teachers are open to change and advice.

The mindset shifts discussed in chapter 4 (establish trust and confidence; avoid hidden agendas; lead the learning; become an insider, not an outsider; know the right things; ensure confidentiality; and know when to use spotlights and supports) are just as important in the post-observation conference as they are in the pre-observation conference. In fact, these mindset shifts potentially play an even larger role during this final stage of the observation and feedback cycle because the tendency of most teachers is to internalize feedback as a statement about the quality of their teaching.

Even the most confident of bilingual and dual-language teachers can find themselves feeling vulnerable during this post-observation conference as they prepare (or brace themselves) to hear what someone else thinks about how they performed. While many bilingual and dual-language teachers trust the observation and feedback cycle during the first three stages, the fourth stage can elicit anxiety and doubt in the fairness of the process.

Share the Data Collected During the Observation

The first step in any model that is going to yield effective feedback is for coaches to share the data they collected during the observation. Teachers must have enough time to review these collected data before the conversation with the coach. This helps reinforce trust, confidence, and transparency. Teacher and coach will have access to the same data, along with an equal opportunity to interpret those data on their own, which reinforces the tone of collaboration rather than a coach preparing to direct the teacher's next steps. Finally, sharing the data helps coaches build confidence in the feedback that's to come by giving teachers the chance to think about why the coach took note of certain things.

Clarify Misconceptions That May Exist in the Coach's Observations

Even as coaches build their understanding and appreciation of the various bilingual and dual-language programs that exist in their buildings, they typically need clarification regarding aspects of what they noticed during their observation. Coaches also need to clarify and understand the what and why behind a range of complex interactions, strategies, and resources. Clarifying possible misconceptions resulting from misinterpretation of the program or language and addressing discrepancies before meeting with the teacher are vital if the coach wants that conversation to be fair and productive. Educators Jana Echevarría, MaryEllen Vogt, and Deborah J. Short (2017) urge those in the position of observer to first work with teachers to get much-needed information that will help contextualize the reason behind certain lesson components and student behaviors.

This insight applies to more than instructional strategies and is important to how coaches approach debriefing and providing feedback. With so many factors to consider, coaches cannot approach these conversations with a singular, one-size-fits-all model. Instead, as coaches share and review the data they collect, they must compare each instructional moment and decision against a range of factors, including "each program's student population, teacher qualifications, and availability of resources in the target language" (Williams, 2015). These three factors can add additional layers and shades of complexity to what coaches observe and help simplify the identification of next steps.

Inquiry and clarification must take place before analysis when a coach observes a lesson in a language he or she doesn't speak. Coaches cannot accurately examine the data they collect for possible high-leverage opportunities when they don't fully comprehend each aspect of the experience. Coaches don't need clarification on everything before the post-observation conference; however, after reviewing the evidence from the noticings with the teacher, they should have a better sense of any additional information they need. Many coaches find they need to ask teachers for clarification because they don't understand the language of instruction, such as how teachers decided to phrase questions during the lesson, what a teacher said before a critical moment in the lesson and why, and any additional context necessary to clarify how each interaction helped students achieve the learning goal.

According to Andrade et al. (1996), when observing in another language, coaches must acknowledge that observations and notes don't perfectly measure teacher effectiveness. Coaches can, however, "hypothesize from the teacher's interactions, missed opportunities, lesson corrections, and adjustments how efficiently teachers work through a range of strategies and tools to ensure student success" (p. 9). Coaches observing in another language must understand that their skill in fairly evaluating a teacher's ability to make decisions that ensure student success is only accurate when coaches fully understand the content of those interactions, corrections, and adjustments that may have been lost in translation or missed in the early stages of the observation and feedback cycle.

That is why inquiry is the catalyst to identifying a teacher's abilities. Coaches can inquire and clarify misconceptions fairly easily by sending a quick email, checking in during grade-level or team meetings, or leaving a note in the teacher's mailbox. The few extra minutes to inquire and clarify can provide a wealth of information that make this step well worth the time.

Identify Trends of Success Regarding Instructional Planning, Delivery, and Assessment

Once coaches have taken the time to inquire about and contextualize the data they collected from the six tasks of notice, they should analyze the data to determine evidence that best captures the efficiency of teachers' problem solving and strategizing to ensure student learning. While this sounds simple, it can be a challenging task. Coaches should not look for or expect simple, single issues that teachers can merely fix with a quick strategy or change of materials.

Bilingual and dual-language classrooms are complex environments that require coaches to look for how each piece fits together, how and why those pieces work, and which trends and turning points create more or less effective outcomes. When looking for such indicators of teaching effectiveness, coaches may locate them lingering below the surface of several different instructional practices. The following list is not exhaustive, but provides a number of key places a coach may look for trends of teaching efficiency.

- The amount of time teachers spend on critical learning versus nonessential learning
- The amount of time teachers devote to student discourse and interaction
- The teacher investing language and content goals with equal status or importance
- The teacher providing various levels of engagement across each chunk of learning
- The teacher employing assessment practices that echo the content, language, and cultural complexities of the classroom

Consider Multiple Cause-and-Effect Relationships

Many coaches find that they see more than one trend or pattern emerge as they go through the previous step of preparing for the post-observation conference. This is to be expected. Teaching and learning in a classroom that serves language learners are complicated. Coaches should aim to understand and analyze which opportunities, interactions, assignments, and teaching methods were effective for students, and for which students specifically they were effective. They must ground these conclusions in the evidence they gather during the tasks of notice.

During this analysis, coaches should first identify effective instructional opportunities, interactions, work samples, and student talk. What are the successes of the lesson, and how do they know? Starting with successes allows coaches to lead with acknowledgment and validation of those complex skills that teachers have already developed and internalized. From there, coaches can consider moments during the lesson that represented challenges, missed opportunities, confusion, or other elements that have the potential to improve. Again, coaches should look for the *why* behind these issues. What preceded that outcome, or what caused that particular result to take place? Was there a clear antecedent or catalyst? Why does that particular action, decision, or instructional approach matter in this situation?

Finally, coaches need to consider the feedback and supports that best address the opportunities, interactions, strategies, and decisions that will help teachers improve the lesson. Therefore, the post-observation conference must engage teachers in a dialogue about problems noticed that require a solution, how accurate teachers were in identifying students' needs, and how successful teachers were in matching the most effective strategy or approach to their students' unique needs.

Verify Earliest Possible Challenges to Use as Leverage Points for the Four Essential Questions

For coaches new to this work, the most efficient strategy is to first consider the evidence collected during the tasks of notice against the first essential question. Coaches must be clear about the one essential question that serves as the focus of their feedback, because they are better able to have a constructive post-observation conference. For example, are safety, equity, and agency present for all students so they can access learning? This essential question is positioned at the macro, or big-picture, level because of its prominent and obvious ability to derail students' ability to learn. When analyzing instruction with this macro view, the coach must prioritize the biggest opportunities the teacher capitalized on or missed as high-leverage changes. The coach can use the four essential questions (see page 72) to provide a sense of confidence in the feedback provided and capacity-building support negotiated during the post-observation conference with the teacher. Should coaches continue to lack confidence in the accuracy and potency of their observations and feedback, they should remember the almost impossible likelihood of a universally correct piece of feedback or capacity-building effort that can guarantee a specific outcome for students.

Coaches can use the essential questions with the abundance of interactions, strategies, opportunities, tools, and adjustments documented during the observation to point them toward the most important feedback to provide to teachers. That is why these questions are essential.

Coaches must provide feedback that will not just improve teacher practice for that one lesson, or lessons that are similar to the one that was observed. Rather, they must choose feedback that will increase the teacher's effectiveness in ways that transfer to other lessons, other content areas, and other times that require a more effective means of problem solving to ensure students are successful. The essential questions represent transferable skills and areas that require problem solving by teachers.

Is the first essential question the most important and the fourth essential question the least important? No, because these questions are all essential. Coaches should consider each essential question as a prerequisite for the next in order for feedback to have the greatest influence on student success. In other words, feedback that coaches provide to teachers about the second essential question will not be as influential in improving outcomes for students if the teacher still must improve his or her practice in the first essential question. When using essential questions in this way, the analysis of cause-and-effect relationships inherent in learning becomes less arduous and yields a more accurate and reliable path forward for teachers to grow.

Four Tasks for the Post-Observation Conference

Regardless of what coaches observe or the leverage points that emerge during their analysis, they must remember to be respectful and insightful, and complete the following four tasks.

1. Name the successes.
2. Guide teachers to reflect on missed opportunities.
3. Agree on one macro-level change, if needed.
4. Collaboratively brainstorm and align strategies that will help teachers achieve their SMART goals and internalize improvements.

Begin the post-observation conference by discussing the successes and instructional opportunities that teachers maximized to increase student learning. It is important to point out successes first. As an example of feedback focused on success, a coach might say, "I noticed the bilingual anchor chart for mathematics. I saw at least six students referring back to it as a resource to complete the task independently. Having that language support readily available facilitated student learning of important mathematics concepts and language development. It's a resource that students seem comfortable using, and I did not observe any of the higher proficiency-level students even looking up." Note that this comment gives equal status to the language and content-area successes, as well as acknowledging the students who can apply their learning and integrate appropriate tools to support their learning independently.

After sharing observations about instructional delivery for students, it is important for coaches to guide bilingual and dual-language teachers through the same type of reflection on instruction that their monolingual colleagues typically do. Asking teachers to discuss their reflections about the success of the lesson against what they intended students to learn in the LOTE across content, language, and culture is a support that bilingual and dual-language teachers welcome. This is an honest and truly reflective discussion about missed learning opportunities relative to a more holistic view of student learning since LOTE data and language acquisition are usually not part of the observation cycle tied to teacher performance. Simple questions like the following can be an effective starting point.

1. How successful was the lesson? Did students learn and apply the content and language goals you planned for them? How do you know?
2. In what ways do student work samples show how students applied learning from the content as well as their new language goals?
3. Do these work samples help show any misunderstandings or misuse of language? In what ways?
4. If you could reteach this lesson, what interactions, strategies, scaffolds, or opportunities would you revise or redo in order to improve student learning in the LOTE?
5. What aspects of your lesson that were *less* effective than what you planned caused you to change your instructional plan? What about those aspects were *more* effective?

The post-observation conference is a time for the coach and the teacher to discuss multiple aspects of the lesson observed. They must discuss those practices, teacher decisions, and student outcomes that were effective and successful. This feedback should begin from the earliest essential question that offered evidence of success. By naming effective practices from prerequisite essential questions, teachers will be better able to connect that success to new learning.

The coach must also provide feedback about those practices, decisions, and student outcomes that are less (or not at all) effective and successful. These are missed opportunities for student success but possible opportunities for teacher improvement. This is the part of the post-observation conference that most often goes awry because of the tendency of many coaches to lose their focus or get bogged down with talk about practices or decisions that have little to do with the essential question selected as a focus.

I have seen a number of post-observation conferences derailed by questions (from both coaches and bilingual and dual-language teachers) about student transfers, lack of materials, attendance issues, and many other concerns. While these may be important issues for discussion, coaches must consider these topics as a distraction from the primary focus of the conference. Coaches can respectfully acknowledge the importance of these issues for the teacher, determine if and when follow-up is needed, and then refocus the conversation on the impact of the teacher's decisions on student learning.

Coaches can maximize this part of the post-observation conference by helping the teacher focus on and analyze just a few key moments from the lesson. Coaches can help teachers analyze these moments by asking simple questions such as:

1. "What happened in this teaching action or practice? What information were you using that led to that action or practice?" (Andrade et al., 1996)
2. "Why did that action or practice take place? What extra information was present but not used in performing that action or practice?" (Andrade et al., 1996)
3. "Are feedback, development, and coaching about that action or practice the best starting point when building a series of improvements? How do you know?"
4. "What do you predict will be the outcome of changing this action or practice?"
5. "What instructional strategies are available that address student challenges?"

Figure 7.1 identifies a number of guiding questions coaches can use as they identify practices and actions that need improvement during the post-observation conference.

Bilingual- and Dual-Language-Specific Supports

The supports that coaches and teachers collaboratively plan represent the necessary steps teachers must take to ensure their path to improvement. These steps must include specific actions and strategies designed to help teachers learn new skills, develop a plan to use those skills, see a model of those skills in action (by connecting other bilingual or dual-language teachers who have mastered specific skills), and receive feedback on their use of these new strategies in action. This is a sort of gradual release of responsibility model often used with students in helping them to own their learning. Teachers can learn using the same model.

However, providing these supports through a gradual release model in a classroom whose students learn in a language that the coach doesn't speak requires much more flexible and creative thinking. Coaches and teachers must work

The Four Essential Questions	Guiding Questions
Are safety, equity, and agency present for all students so they can access learning?	1. In what ways do all students show that they feel safe, like they belong, and that they have social, emotional, and behavioral support? 2. How might the teacher use cultural differences as learning opportunities to teach students about cultural differences, clarify misconceptions, and validate identity? 3. How does the teacher develop rules, power dynamics, and expectations to reflect the dimensions of culture unique to the student demographic? 4. Do teacher-student and student-student interactions demonstrate respect and the conditions needed by all learners to be valued and successful? 5. Do all students experience high expectations, meaningful engagement, and feedback around learning and behavior within the learning community?
Is there a community of respect that maximizes instructional time and focus?	1. What cultural preferences does the teacher consider in organizing the classroom, defining cooperation, defining the importance of time to learn, grouping students, and maximizing the room for engagement and interaction? 2. How does the teacher use language, scaffolds, and a range of adaptations strategically to ensure all students understand what they are learning across content, language, and culture? 3. In what ways does the teacher provide access to first language and background knowledge to students in order to maximize language growth and content learning? 4. In what ways does the teacher use learning, language, and culture during instruction in a way that is appropriate for language learners? 5. What authentic formative assessments of content, language, and literacy drive the planning process and development of appropriate rubrics? 6. Does the lesson provide the right amount and quality of feedback to ensure students continue their progress?

continued →

Figure 7.1: Post-observation guiding questions for coaches.

Visit go.SolutionTree.com/EL for a free reproducible version of this figure.

The Four Essential Questions	Guiding Questions
Does the instructional design help students master rigorous content, acquire more complex academic language, think critically about relevant uses, and build independence?	1. How does students' learning of content, language, and skills reflect the essential learning for their grade level? 2. Are there sufficient supports (sensory, graphic, or interactive) that are a true match to students' real-time proficiency levels and background knowledge, or would the teacher change the materials if he or she could redo the lesson? 3. How are students able to apply learning in ways that allow them practice in meaningful and authentic contexts—for example, read books in original Spanish instead of translated texts, practice fractions through recipes, or practice new language structures through content-based conversations? 4. How does the teacher vary questioning, discussion techniques, and interactions to maximize language models, language use, and engagement in learning by all students regardless of proficiency or native language? 5. How do students communicate what they know and are able to do along a range of higher-order thinking and depths of knowledge—for example, using and showing reasoning skills within their language abilities—at a range of proficiency levels without the teacher watering down the curriculum? 6. In what ways does the teacher provide all students with varied opportunities for meaningful discourse and critical thinking in content learning while providing necessary adaptations and scaffolds for language proficiency and comprehensible input?
Are the practices, skills, and strategies observed accurately implemented and aligned to the program's vision and goals?	1. How are the practices, resources, and language usage essential to the vision of this program? Does the teacher know of other practices that could further the broader vision within this lesson? 2. How are students owning, developing, and self-assessing their specific content and language goals that represent their stretch learning, or learning just outside of their comfort zone? 3. How does the teacher use and interpret data to ensure an accurate picture of learning progress, cross-linguistic connections, and accurate conclusions for support, intervention, and acceleration? 4. How does the teacher adjust the pacing, lesson structure, and unit components to ensure every student achieves grade-level and program goals?

together to brainstorm and map out a specific coaching plan that helps teachers access new learning and support its application in a language other than English.

Supports for that new learning that a coach may suggest include the following.

- Local and national workshops that are now offered in multiple languages
- Recommended texts that build the necessary conceptual knowledge
- Other bilingual and dual-language teachers in the building
- District specialists
- Highly effective bilingual and dual-language teachers in nearby schools using the same (not similar) model
- Coordination of teacher-to-teacher observations with other well-established programs
- Districtwide bilingual and dual-language professional learning communities (PLCs)
- Monolingual teachers who are able to effectively develop or co-plan for new skills, even if they don't model its use in their own classroom

These supports, among others, are key to developing a plan that can solidify a teacher's successful implementation of new strategies and skills. Accordingly, at the end of the post-observation conference, neither the coach nor teacher leaves the table without key responsibilities and next steps intentionally designed to improve student success.

The coach must be sure to identify what role she or he and the school will play in providing teachers with opportunities to learn the new strategies and skills (for example, articles, videos, models, workshops, conferences, or other cohorts throughout the district). Will the school need to secure funds for the teacher to go to a conference? Will they need to purchase books or other resources? Will they need to request substitutes for the teacher to be released to observe another teacher, and if so, from which budget will they pay that substitute? These are the details that require careful follow-through by the coach.

In the case of providing bilingual and dual-language-specific supports, taking a singular (in this case, monolingual) stance and placing value on what is right, wrong, or in need of correction, coaches should invite teachers to discuss what actions they could take to improve student learning. In other words, the coach must speculate which actions are most likely to yield accelerated growth for teachers and students. And what's more, why do these actions have the potential for ultimate impact?

Following are seven supports that are unique to bilingual and dual-language teachers and classrooms.

1. The curriculum resources and materials in the LOTE provide meaningful opportunities to master content objectives, language objectives, oracy, print literacy, and opportunities to develop academic and social language across both program languages. Materials reflect the diversity of the language and cultures, a variety of genres, authentic literature, and a variety of visual materials in both program languages.

2. The curriculum has a well-defined scope and sequence for initial and more advanced literacy in the LOTE or one that specifically addresses the literacy skills necessary to read and write in that language rather than simply mirroring the teaching of English literacy.

3. Instructional planning processes and planning tools (for example, lesson- and unit-planning templates) support and foster the use of thematic, cross-disciplinary, or project-based approaches and use a variety of techniques that respond to different language proficiency levels and various learning styles, including visuals, models, alternative assessments, comprehensible speech, scaffolds, and presentations as well as other strategies that teachers utilize during instructional delivery.

4. The district and school offer regular times for educators to vertically and horizontally align the curriculum to link content and language across languages and grades.

5. The district and school support bilingual and dual-language teachers in identifying, acquiring, and determining the most effective conditions for providing interventions across both languages so emergent bilinguals can receive interventions in their first language based on literacy trajectories that teachers have developed for other bilingual and dual-language students rather than using monolingual benchmarks that don't speak to the additional demands placed on these classrooms.

6. Schools provide clear expectations, time, training, resources, modeling, and feedback to implement ongoing professional learning and develop effective improvement cycles. This learning includes instructional design as well as classroom management skills, cultural proficiency, and training for additional staff who interact with the students whom bilingual and dual-language classrooms serve.

7. Groups of teachers meet on a regular basis to provide feedback to one another and assist in refining their teaching (Echevarría et al., 2017).

With teachers, coaches can co-create an explicit plan that identifies how the teachers will learn new strategies, the time line of that learning, and opportunities to observe a model lesson (in their classroom or another class in the same program) in the LOTE. At the end of that learning plan, teachers and coaches must take the time to reflect on how successful the plan was in improving student learning. They might reflect on the following questions.

- What is the subsequent support plan and natural cycle of how teachers will learn, practice, and incorporate that support?
- What are the activities that will define that support plan with responsibilities for both parties?
- How will both parties define increased student learning and know when to celebrate when they succeed?

Plan for Success

Most coaches who begin their journey in observing and providing feedback for bilingual and dual-language teachers find how quickly they are able to improve the accuracy and efficiency of the entire cycle so they can focus on this last part of the post-observation conference—putting a plan together.

Figure 7.2 (page 114) provides coaches with a tool to plan and organize a step-by-step coaching plan with teachers, including evidence analyzed from the observation to determine how effective that support plan will be.

This tool helps coaches and bilingual and dual-language teachers focus on just one essential question—the one that represents the earliest identified area of challenge. Then the coach is able to identify the evidence from the observation and the guiding questions to ask prior to the post-observation conference. During this conference, the coach and teacher will develop a plan to improve instruction.

In the Plan section, coaches can note the strategies that they discussed with teachers during the pre-observation conference. They then review any evidence they collect that speaks to the strategies planned, as well as additional evidence of each essential question in action. Coaches can note this evidence in the Evidence section. Below that, coaches can outline possible questions to ask during the post-observation conference as they identify the most effective leverage points for improvement. They can also use these questions while facilitating teachers' reflection on the effectiveness of their instructional decisions.

Conclusion

To create a fair process that transforms outcomes for bilingual and dual-language teachers, what happens after the observation is just as important as what happens during the observation. Even though the tasks of notice are designed to focus on the observable, regardless of language, coaches still need to analyze the evidence

Essential Question 1: Are safety, equity, and agency present for all students so they can access learning?	
Plan	
Evidence	
Reflection Questions	

Essential Question 2: Is there a community of respect that maximizes instructional time and focus?	
Plan	
Evidence	
Reflection Questions	

Essential Question 3: Does the instructional design help students master rigorous content, acquire more complex academic language, think critically about relevant uses, and build independence?	
Plan	
Evidence	
Reflection Questions	

Essential Question 4: Are the practices, skills, and strategies observed accurately implemented and aligned to the program's vision and goals?	
Plan	
Evidence	
Reflection Questions	

Figure 7.2: Evidence of the four essential questions.

*Visit **go.SolutionTree.com/EL** for a free reproducible version of this figure.*

through a collaborative process. This collaboration must take place while preparing for the actual observation and the post-observation conference, and in planning for supports and actions.

Coaching bilingual and dual-language teachers is critical to improving student outcomes. However, effectively coaching these teachers requires shifts in mindset, thinking, approach, and feedback. These shifts are necessary to ensure that all teachers and their students have the ability to achieve their full potential.

Coaches can use the "Action-Planning Template" reproducible (page 116) to help organize the learning from this chapter into smaller, more easily accomplished goals.

Chapter 7: Action-Planning Template

Use this chart to help you organize the learning from this chapter into smaller, more easily accomplished goals.

Next Steps	Time Line	Resources
1.		
2.		
3.		
4.		
5.		
6.		
7.		
8.		
9.		

APPENDIX A

Bilingual and Dual-Language Programs

Table A.1: Bilingual Programs

Bilingual Programs		
Transitional Bilingual Education		**Transitional Program of Instruction**
Early Exit	**Late Exit**	**English as a Second (New) Language Programs or English to Speakers of Other Languages**
In many states, once a school enrolls more than twenty language learners of the same language background (all Spanish speaking or Arabic speaking), they must offer a bilingual program. Transitional bilingual classrooms are labeled that way because their goal is to transition all students in the classroom to being fully proficient in English. Kindergarten classrooms generally begin with almost all their core instruction in the first language of the students enrolled in the class. Each year, students transition into greater amounts of their core instruction being delivered in English. The final transition to English only happens around second or third grade for early exit programs and around fourth or fifth grades for late exit programs.		Language specialists either push in to the general education classroom or pull students out of the general education classroom to teach language learners from a variety of language backgrounds and often leverage native language during instruction for language learners early in their English acquisition.
Basic Features: Additive or Subtractive	**Basic Features: Additive or Subtractive**	**Basic Features: Additive or Subtractive**
Students come from the same non-English language background. The amount of LOTE used decreases each year until students reach English-only instruction—usually by around second grade. This is a subtractive model, as the goal is to transition the LOTE out and replace it with all English.	Students come from the same non-English language background. The amount of LOTE used decreases each year until students reach English-only instruction—usually in third through fifth grade. This is a subtractive model, as the goal is to transition the LOTE out and replace it with all English.	Students don't always come from the same non-English language background. Teachers are encouraged to use students' first language as a support for students who have recently arrived or are still new to English. However, from the very beginning, these programs are designed to be English-only instruction. This is the most subtractive model, as the goal is to replace their current language abilities with all English as quickly as possible.

Source: Lindholm-Leary, 2001; Soltero, 2016; Thomas & Collier, 2012.

117

Table A.2: Dual-Language Programs

Dual-Language Programs			
Whole-School Options		**Strand-Within-a-Building Options**	
Dual-Language Education			
Developmental Bilingual Program	**Two-Way Immersion Program**	**Foreign Language Immersion Program**	**Heritage Language Program**
Also sometimes called *one-way program*	Also sometimes called *dual-language immersion, two-way dual-language*, or *bilingual immersion*	Also sometimes called *one-way immersion*	Also sometimes called *language restoration and maintenance*
Program Students	**Program Students**	**Program Students**	**Program Students**
English learners (EL) who share the same native language make up 100 percent of the students in the program.	There is a balance between EL-identified and target language students (the non-English program language like Spanish, Chinese, Arabic, or French).	More than 67 percent of the students speak English.	Heritage language learners (HLL) make up 100 percent of the students (HLLs have some foundation in the language or connection to the culture "through family, community, or country of origin" [Center for Applied Linguistics, 2016]).
Basic Features: Additive or Enrichment	**Basic Features: Additive or Enrichment**	**Basic Features: Additive or Enrichment**	**Basic Features: Additive or Enrichment**
Goal: Bilingualism, biliteracy, and multicultural competence **Characteristics:** Typically offered at grades preK–5 and ideally preK–12 in which language and core content instruction are integrated, with at least half the instruction provided in the non-English program language	**Goal:** Bilingualism, biliteracy, and multicultural competence **Characteristics:** A balance of English-speaking and English-learning students learn together and from one another; core content instruction is delivered in the two program languages, resulting in an equal valuing of the two languages; typically results in language equity rather than language loss	**Goal:** Bilingualism, biliteracy, and multicultural competence **Characteristics:** Typically offered in preK–5 as an enrichment; content instruction is delivered across two program languages; typically results in bilingualism and biliteracy but a low biculturalism result	**Goal:** Avoid language loss, re-establish cultural identity, and develop high levels of bilingualism and biliteracy. **Characteristics:** Typically offered at grades 6–12 in which classes tap into the strengths and needs of heritage learners, who are different than students in foreign or world-language classes who may not have grown up around the language

Program Models or Language Allocation (Distribution) Plan			
90:10	**80:20**	**50:50**	**Alternating**
Students are immersed for 90 percent of the time in the target or partner language for the first one to two years and then gradually increase the percentage of English until it reaches a balance of 50:50 by grade 5. The 10 percent of English instruction is focused on English language development (or ELD) through a focus on oral language supported by well-trained ESL teachers.	This is typically an adaptation of the 90:10 model with the larger percentage of the time still being in the target or partner language in the early years, then increasing in English until it reaches a balance of 50:50 by grade 5. The 20 percent of English instruction in the early years of the program must still include ELD delivered by well-trained ESL teachers but can also include a range of other content areas or classes, depending on each school's focus and staff makeup.	Students spend 50 percent of the time in the target language and 50 percent of the time in English beginning in kindergarten. Students don't just learn each language, but also literacy and proficiency, and master the required content (such as mathematics, science, and social studies) in both languages simultaneously.	This is typically an adaptation of the 50:50 model with students still spending about 50 percent of the time in the target language and 50 percent of the time in English. Schools might alternate the schedule in a variety of ways to achieve this balance, including: alternating morning and afternoon (one classroom spends their morning with their Mandarin dual-language teacher and then switches with the other class so they spend their afternoon with their English dual-language teacher), alternating days, and sometimes alternating weeks or units.

Benefits:
- 90:10 models help build a stronger foundation in oral language, literacy skills, and critical vocabulary before transferring that foundation to English.
- Students in 90:10 models show accelerated progress in productive English because they have already developed literacy skills in the target language (Paradis, Genesee, & Crago, 2004).
- Students in 90:10 models often close the achievement gap faster than those in 50:50 models.
- Some schools implementing 50:50 models find greater community support and sufficient student and family enrollment.
- Schools implementing 50:50 models find the task of recruiting, hiring, and retaining quality bilingual teachers more manageable.

Challenges:
- 90:10 models often struggle to recruit, hire, and retain sufficient educators for the duration of the program.
- Leaders of 90:10 models find it difficult to support teacher capacity-building efforts without much-needed training and tend to place additional demands of translating, using English for English-speaking students rather than those teaching strategies that make language accessible, and overlook the needs of these teachers during grade-level planning meetings.
- 50:50 models often struggle to meaningfully connect the two languages since there are often two teachers—one for each of the languages.
- There is a tendency for 50:50 models to implement curricula that are quite repetitive. Without clear coordination and without repetition of what students are learning in each language, students risk receiving less content and essential standards than their monolingual peers.

Source: Lindholm-Leary, 2001; Soltero, 2016; Thomas & Collier, 2012.

Frequently Asked Questions

Following are some common questions coaches and teachers often ask about the observation and feedback cycle.

1. I still don't feel it's fair to observe when instruction is in another language. Can any person truly do this effectively?

Coaches are right to be cautious about maintaining fairness and professionalism, especially if the school will ultimately use the observation for purposes of teacher evaluation. And, in truth, many educators worry about the risk inherent in a process that places judgment on something taking place in a language they don't understand. Sometimes, coaches are joined by bilingual and dual-language teachers themselves who also worry about the process (see question 4).

Even still, it's hard to stop wondering about the almost invisible, and mostly unintentional, double standard of this question. Observing, collecting evidence, and providing feedback for teacher improvement and learning are at the heart of teacher excellence. Many districts have provided some form of coaching to new, novice, and struggling teachers for years. It is only fair to provide those supports to bilingual and dual-language teachers as they work to implement new programs, create a range of resources and materials in each of the program languages, and support students as they learn the content areas and another language. In order to improve outcomes for students, we have to accept the reality that we have more bilingual students than teachers, and more bilingual teachers than academic coaches. Through practice and true collaboration, however, all teachers can have access to the support they need to develop their craft and improve outcomes for all students.

2. But isn't this all just good instruction? Aren't these supports good for all students?

Providing good instruction is effective for all students. However, for bilingual and dual-language students, these practices are essential in order for students to access the education promise of various program models. Without close attention to these practices, students are likely to encounter insurmountable barriers that seriously impact their ability to make sense of grade-level content, two languages, biliteracy, and meaningful concepts or skills necessary to develop into engaged and critical thinkers who are ready for college, career, and beyond.

3. I know most programs ask students and teachers to stay in the language of instruction. Is it all right if I talk with students during an observation or ask them questions if I can only do it in English?

Absolutely. Is it better to engage with students in the program language of the day in order to ensure continuity and flow? Yes, however, engaging with students to explore learning from their perspective is absolutely critical. So engaging with them in any language is better than not interacting with them at all.

4. I have tried to coach my bilingual and dual-language teachers, but they don't seem very receptive. Is there something I can do?

Even though it sounds like a pretty straightforward question, the heart of the issue is likely to be quite complex. For this reason, I hesitate to ever give one overgeneralized answer when I hear this question. In truth, it just depends. More often than not, because matters of language acquisition come with issues of power, access, politics, national immigration policies, competing funding sources, and a range of limiting beliefs, there could be a number of complex issues looming under the surface.

One of the significant challenges at play tends to be issues of trust. At times, bilingual and dual-language teachers may show reluctance that stems from a lack of trust in the motives of this new effort or focus if it is not clearly communicated with transparency. Distrust might also be a by-product of harsh lessons learned over the course of their careers as they have been observed, misunderstood, and provided with feedback that did little to acknowledge and support the roles that language and culture have on the instructional decision-making process. These painful experiences can cause bilingual and dual-language teachers to both fear and be skeptical of any future coach's ability to be objective and constructive during the coaching cycle.

We must also reflect on our school systems beyond these two shared experiences of many bilingual and dual-language educators. Most schools provide some combination of services like leadership coaching, curricular resources, continuous professional development, authentic assessments, systems for early identification of necessary supports, and more, as they should. However, for a number of reasons, most of these supports take place in English and with little consideration for how they might not be the best approach for students learning English or an entirely different language that has its own structure and developmental stages.

After a while, many bilingual and dual-language teachers with few tools and inconsistent supports can become distrustful of the system that holds them accountable for the same growth and results as their monolingual colleagues without acknowledging this inequity. They are used to feeling insecure, that they are at risk of being misinterpreted and misunderstood. Only time, transparency, recognition, and effective communication will help bilingual and dual-language educators move past these critical issues.

5. We have a dual-language program in our district for Spanish and Chinese. We know they're both different from English, but shouldn't I be looking for the same best practices?

An essential distinction for us all to understand is what the term *best practice* means. There are some practices, techniques, or instructional moves that produce greater results than their alternatives. John Hattie's (2012) research analysis centers on the question of what those practices are and which ones lead to the greatest result. Some of the practices with the highest effect size according to his research include formative assessment, feedback, metacognitive strategies, direct instruction, questioning techniques, writing, and cooperative learning. These practices are undoubtedly good for all students.

However, these practices by themselves are not sufficient to produce equal impact or similar effect with language learners. This is because in bilingual and dual-language classrooms, factors—such as the program model, the balance between direct instruction and differentiated instruction, vocabulary instruction, strategic scaffolding aligned to students' language development, the use of visual aids, the ways in which oral language is developed and leveraged to achieve higher levels of print literacy, and access to technology to bridge the gap of resources and access to authentic experiences with language—play just as vital a role in providing students with opportunities to acquire and apply newly learned skills in the context of meaningful interaction inside and outside the classroom.

What's more, and especially as it relates to literacy instruction, we must understand how the two languages students are navigating are different and what to do about those differences. A prime example of this is the use of English word walls organized in alphabetical order as a way to help students develop a bank of sight words. Since the words' initial letter sound (or phoneme) represents one of the major cueing systems for readers, this organization makes sense.

However, the initial letter sound (or phoneme) organized by the alphabet is not a major cueing system in Spanish. It doesn't provide any significant support to students as they encounter words they don't know and have to problem solve as a reader. Unlike English, Spanish phonemes (or sounds) are some of the most transparent of all languages. The letter *a* is pronounced the same every time. The sound doesn't change if there is an *e* or a *y* at the end or if the word has a consonant-vowel-consonant-vowel (CVCV) pattern. It is pronounced the same every single time. That's why word walls are not recommended in classrooms where Spanish literacy is taught. Providing explicit instruction in comprehension, phonics and decoding, vocabulary, fluency, and the necessary background knowledge (August & Shannahan, 2006) is necessary if we want students to become fully bilingual and biliterate. Yet, how we teach these core areas to maintain the cultural and linguistic integrity of each language within our district must be of the highest priority.

6. How can I get more practice observing and providing feedback before going into the classroom?

You can practice and refine your skills in a variety of ways and places. One accessible opportunity is to view videos of lessons that teachers in your own building conduct in a language you don't speak before they are scheduled to engage in the observation and feedback cycle. In addition, many coaches find that forming teams where they are able to practice, observe, and collaborate on effective feedback across a range of classrooms and buildings is a huge help.

One consideration, however, is whether teachers are ready for this type of practice if the school year has already started. In cases where trust is an issue, summer school classes might provide a better option since they typically fall outside of high-stakes evaluation timeframes. In these situations, summer school classrooms might offer the same access to instruction and practice without the fear of any potential influence on formal evaluations that take place during the school year.

7. During my pre-observation conference, how can I make sure that I am discussing data accurately so I know which students are learning and which students might need additional support?

This is an important question and one coaches don't ask enough. Discussing data accurately is a skill that many coaches have developed as it pertains to literacy or content data. Use that ability as a starting point. Consider the ways you discuss whole-group and individual needs with teachers, and how the plan for instruction speaks to students' needs. These are powerful moves. Accurately discussing data begins by knowing the language of instruction for the content area you are discussing. In other words, if you only teach literacy in Spanish, then you should prioritize Spanish literacy data.

The conversation also must include language and culture. Coaches must learn how teachers have determined students' language proficiency and how they used that information to drive the lesson and embedded scaffolds. They also must determine how teachers learned about students' background knowledge to match appropriate resources and minimize errors that come from cultural differences. The information that we learn about students must be reliable enough to use meaningfully. This is a skill that takes both time and practice to develop.

8. What about the first one or two weeks of school? Teachers want to start in English to establish routines and then begin implementing the program model. I want every classroom to have positive and engaged learning communities, so is this practice appropriate?

Some new programs have begun to institute this process. However, there is no research to support or disprove it. We know that the language a teacher uses to establish the culture and norms of the classroom will forever be branded as the default language, or language used when other academic demands require more work from students. This is, perhaps, the greatest danger of using English as the foundation and then changing the expectation for students. From my own observations and that of many colleagues in the field, we find programs that maintain the language of instruction from the very start of school are most successful at establishing credibility for that language and the grit that students will need to comprehend instruction, provided the right supports are in place. The exception to maintaining the language of instruction is the presence of an emergency. In this case, language and content mastery become secondary to student safety and well-being.

9. What are the most important things I should be looking for in a lesson plan?

It is challenging to narrow down a lesson plan to a few key components. However, the following six components are absolutely essential for emergent bilinguals to realize academic and linguistic success.

1. Resources and an environment that supports their learning across all goals (content, language, and culture)
2. Clear content that reflects rigorous grade-level learning, and language students will learn and use across varied domains
3. Opportunities to connect learning and language to background knowledge and a range of experiences
4. Varied opportunities to collaborate with others
5. Formative and summative self-reflection and assessments that get at the heart of what students know and are able to do

6. Engaging opportunities for students to apply what they've learned across all three goals (content, language, and culture) through extension or creation of something meaningful

10. Do the research, practices, and processes offered in this book align to Guiding Principles for Dual Language Education (GP3; Howard et al., 2018), since it is the most commonly used resource for implementing and continuously improving bilingual and dual-language programs?

The research, practices, and processes that this text offers rely heavily on the same body of research that Howard et al. (2018) used in developing the GP3. However, because this book is meant for a broader audience, GP3 was not the sole reference for leverage. Those implementing the most commonly used program models (developmental bilingual or two-way immersion) in the United States will see the natural connections to the seven strands in the guide: (1) program structure, (2) curriculum, (3) instruction, (4) assessment and accountability, (5) staff quality and professional development, (6) family and community, and (7) support and resources. However, those who are not implementing those specific program models will appreciate the alternative method to observing and identifying powerful feedback, the broader research basis, and the practicality of tools that can be matched to the program model itself, instead of the other way around.

References and Resources

Aguilar, E. (2013). *The art of coaching: Effective strategies for school transformation.* San Francisco: Jossey-Bass.

American Educational Research Association. (2014). *Standards for educational and psychological testing.* Washington, DC: Author.

Andrade, A. M., Basurto, A. G. M., Clay, M., Ruiz, O. A., & Escamilla, K. (1996). *Instrumento de observación de los logros de la lecto-escritura inicial: Spanish reconstruction of* An Observation Survey, *a bilingual text.* Portsmouth, NH: Heinemann.

Athanases, S. Z., & de Oliveira, L. C. (2008). Advocacy for equity in classrooms and beyond: New teachers' challenges and responses. *Teachers College Record, 110*(1), 64–104.

August, D., & Hakuta, K. (1997). *Improving schooling for language-minority children: A research agenda.* Washington, DC: National Academies Press.

August, D., & Shanahan, T. (Eds.). (2006). *Developing literacy in second-language learners: Report of the National Literacy Panel on Language—Minority Children and Youth.* Mahwah, NJ: Erlbaum.

Berducci, D. (1993). Inside the SLA classroom: Verbal interaction in three SL classes. *The Language Learning Journal, 8*(1), 12–16.

Bruce, K. L., Lara-Alecio, R., Parker, R. I, Hasbrouck, J. E., Weaver, L., & Irby, B. (1997). Inside transitional bilingual classrooms: Accurately describing the language learning process. *Bilingual Research Journal, 21*(2–3), 123–145.

Bryk, A. S., Gomez, L. M., Grunow, A., & Lemahieu, P. G. (2015). *Learning to improve: How America's schools can get better at getting better.* Cambridge, MA: Harvard Education Press.

Carlo, M. S., August, D., McLaughlin, B., Snow, C. E., Dressler, C., Lippman, D. N., et al. (2004). Closing the gap: Addressing the vocabulary needs of English-language learners in bilingual and mainstream classrooms. *Reading Research Quarterly, 39*(2), 188–215.

Carnock, J. T., & Garcia, A. (2016, April 21). *Dual immersion programs: How states foster expansion, face challenges* [Blog post]. Accessed at www.newamerica.org/education -policy/edcentral/di-states on March 13, 2019.

CAST. (2018). *Universal design for learning guidelines version 2.2* [Graphic organizer]. Wakefield, MA: Author.

Center for Applied Linguistics. (2016). *Heritage FAQs.* Accessed at www.cal.org /heritage/research/faqs.html#2 on March 14, 2019.

Cloud, N., Genesee, F., & Hamayan, E. (2000). *Dual language instruction: A handbook for enriched education.* Boston: Heinle & Heinle.

Collier, V. P., & Thomas, W. P. (2004). The astounding effectiveness of dual language education for all. *NABE Journal of Research and Practice, 2*(1), 1–20.

Covey, S. R. (1989). *The seven habits of highly effective people: Powerful lessons for personal change.* New York: Free Press.

Crane, E. W. (2010). *Building an interim assessment system: A workbook for school districts.* Accessed at www.wested.org/online_pubs/Interim_Workbook081810.pdf on March 13, 2019.

Cummins, J. (2000). Academic language learning, transformative pedagogy, and information technology: Towards a critical balance. *TESOL Quarterly, 34*(3), 537–548.

Danielson, C. (2001). New trends in teacher evaluation. *Educational Leadership, 58*(5), 12–15.

Danielson, C. (2007). *Enhancing professional practice: A framework for teaching* (2nd ed.). Alexandria, VA: Association for Supervision and Curriculum Development.

Danielson, C. (2011). *The framework for teaching evaluation instrument.* Princeton, NJ: Danielson Group.

Danielson, C. (2013). *The framework for teaching evaluation instrument.* Princeton, NJ: Danielson Group.

Danielson, C., & McGreal, T. L. (2000). *Teacher evaluation to enhance professional practice.* Alexandria, VA: Association for Supervision and Curriculum Development.

DeWitt, P. (2014, November 6). *5 reasons we need instructional coaches* [Blog post]. Accessed at https://blogs.edweek.org/edweek/finding_common_ground/2014/11/5 _reasons_we_need_instructional_coaches.html on March 13, 2019.

Doherty, K. M., & Jacobs, S. (2015). *State of the states: Evaluating teaching, leading, and learning.* Washington, DC: National Council on Teacher Quality.

Dunne, K., & Villani, S. (2007). Preparing mentor teachers as collaborative coaches. In *Mentoring new teachers through collaborative coaching: Linking teacher and student learning* (pp. 55–79). San Francisco: WestEd. Accessed at www.wested.org/online _pubs/LI-06-04_chap4sampleall.pdf on September 2, 2019.

Echevarría, J., & Short, D. J. (2004). Using multiple perspectives in observations of diverse classrooms: The Sheltered Instruction Observation Protocol (SIOP). In H. C. Waxman, R. G. Tharp, & R. S. Hilberg (Eds.), *Observational research in U.S. classrooms: New approaches for understanding cultural and linguistic diversity* (pp. 21–47). Cambridge, England: Cambridge University Press.

Echevarría, J., Vogt, M., & Short, D. J. (2017). *Making content comprehensible for English language learners: The SIOP model* (5th ed.). Boston: Allyn & Bacon.

Edmonds, L. M. (2009). Challenges and solutions for ELLs: Teaching strategies for English Language Learners' success in science. *Science Teacher, 76*(3), 30–33.

Eisenberg, E. B., Eisenberg, B. P., Medrich, E. A., & Charner, I. (2017). *Instructional coaching in action: An integrated approach that transforms thinking, practice, and schools.* Alexandria, VA: Association for Supervision and Curriculum Development.

Escamilla, K., & Andrade, A. (1992). Descubriendo la lectura: An application of reading recovery in Spanish. *Education and Urban Society, 24*(2), 212–226.

Escamilla, K., Hopewell, S., Butvilofsky, S., Sparrow, W., Soltero-González, L., Ruiz-Figueroa, O., et al. (2013). *Biliteracy from the start: Literacy squared in action.* Philadelphia: Caslon.

Fenner, D. S., Kozik, P., & Cooper, A. (2014). Evaluating teachers of all learners. *Leadership, 43*(4), 8–12.

Fox, K. R., Campbell, M., & Hargrove, T. (2011). Examining reflective practice: Insights from pre-service teachers, in-service teachers, and faculty. *Journal of Research in Education, 21*(2), 37–54.

Freeman, R. D. (1998). *Bilingual education and social change.* Clevedon, England: Dual-Language and Bilingual Matters.

Fortune, T. W. (2014). *Immersion teaching strategies observation checklist.* Accessed at http://carla.umn.edu/immersion/checklist.pdf on March 14, 2019.

García, O., Johnson, S. I., & Seltzer, K. (2017). *The translanguaging classroom: Leveraging student bilingualism for learning.* Philadelphia: Caslon.

Gee, J. (2008). A sociocultural perspective on opportunity to learn. In P. Moss, D. Pullin, J. Gee, E. Haertel, & L. Young (Eds.), *Assessment, equity, and opportunity to learn* (pp. 76–108). Cambridge, MA: Cambridge University Press.

Genesee, F., Lindholm-Leary, K., Saunders, W., & Christian, D. (2006). *Educating English language learners: A synthesis of research evidence.* New York: Cambridge University Press.

Gersten, R., Baker, S. K., Shanahan, T., Linan-Thompson, S., Collins, P., & Scarcella, R. (2007). *Effective literacy and English language instruction for English learners in the elementary grades: A practice guide* (NCEE 2007-4011). Washington, DC: National Center for Education Evaluation and Regional Assistance.

Gibbons, P. (2002). *Scaffolding language, scaffolding learning: Teaching second language learners in the mainstream classroom.* Portsmouth, NH: Heinemann.

Gibbons, P. (2009). *English learners academic literacy and thinking: Learning in the challenge zone.* Portsmouth, NH: Heinemann.

Gibbons, P. (2015). *Scaffolding language, scaffolding learning: Teaching second language learners in the mainstream classroom* (2nd ed.). Portsmouth, NH: Heinemann.

Goleman, D. (1995). *Emotional intelligence.* New York: Bantam Books.

Good, T. L., & Brophy, J. E. (1969). *Analyzing classroom interaction: A more powerful alternative.* Austin: Research and Development Center for Teacher Education, University of Texas at Austin.

Gottlieb, M., & Hamayan, E. (2007). Assessing oral and written language proficiency: A guide for psychologists and teachers. In G. B. Esquivel, E. C. Lopez, & S. G. Nahari (Eds.), *Handbook of multicultural school psychology: An interdisciplinary perspective* (pp. 245–263). New York: Erlbaum.

Gottlieb, M., Katz, A., & Ernst-Slavit, G. (2009). *Paper to practice: Using the English language proficiency standards in preK–12 classrooms.* Alexandria, VA: Teachers of English to Speakers of Other Languages.

Grant, C. A. (1989). Equity, equality, teachers, and classroom life. In W. G. Secada (Ed.), *Equity in education* (pp. 89–102). New York: Falmer.

Hamayan, E., & Freeman, R. F. (Eds). (2006). *English language learners at school: A guide for administrators.* Philadelphia: Caslon.

Harris, V. R., & Sandoval-Gonzalez, A. (2017, June). *Unveiling California's growing bilingual teacher shortage: Addressing the urgent shortage, and aligning the workforce to advances in pedagogy and practice in bilingual education.* Accessed at https://californianstogether.org/product/unveiling-californias-growing-bilingual-teacher-shortage-addressing-the-urgent-shortage-and-aligning-the-workforce-to-advances-in-pedagogy-and-practice-in-bilingual-education on March 14, 2019.

Harry, B., Kalyanpur, M., & Day, M. (1999). *Building cultural reciprocity with families.* Baltimore: Paul H. Brookes.

Harry, B., Rueda, R., & Kalyanpur, M. (1999). Cultural reciprocity in sociocultural perspective: Adapting the normalization principle for family collaboration. *Exceptional Children, 66*(1), 123–136.

Hattie, J. (2009). *Visible learning: A synthesis of over 800 meta-analyses relating to achievement.* New York: Routledge.

Hattie, J. (2012). *Visible learning for teachers: Maximizing impact on learning.* New York: Routledge.

Hattie, J., & Timperley, H. (2007). The power of feedback. *Review of Educational Research, 77*(1), 81–112.

Heras, A. (1994). The construction of understanding in a sixth-grade classroom. *Linguistics and Education, 5*(3–4), 275–299.

Heritage, M. (2008). *Learning progressions: Supporting instruction and formative assessment.* Washington, DC: Council of Chief State School Officers.

Heritage, M. (2011, Spring). Formative assessment: An enabler of learning. *Better Evidence-Based Education.* Accessed at www.cse.ucla.edu/products/misc/bettermagazineheritage.pdf on September 4, 2019.

Heritage, M., Walqui, A., & Linquanti, R. (2012, August). *Formative assessment as contingent teaching and learning: Perspectives on assessment as and for language learning in the content areas.* Paper prepared for the Understanding Language conference, Stanford University, CA.

Higher Educators in Linguistically Diverse Education. (2015). *Colorado state model educator evaluation system: Practical ideas for evaluating general education teachers of bilingual learners.* Denver: Colorado Department of Education. Accessed at www.cde.state.co.us/educatoreffectiveness/practicalideaguidebilingual on March 14, 2019.

Hillsborough County Public Schools. (n.d.). *Pre-observation conference guide.* Accessed at http://tntp.org/assets/tools/HCPS%20Pre-Observation%20Conference%20Guide_TSLT%203.12.pdf on March 5, 2019.

Hopkinson, A. (2017, January 6). A new era for bilingual education: Explaining California's Proposition 58. *EdSource.* Accessed at https://edsource.org/2017/a-new-era-for-bilingual-education-explaining-californias-proposition-58/574852 on March 14, 2019.

Howard, E. R., & Christian, D. (2002). *Two-way immersion 101: Designing and implementing a two-way immersion education program at the elementary level.* Santa Cruz, CA: Center for Research in Education, Diversity and Excellence. Accessed at www.cal.org/twi/pdfs/two-way-immersion-101.pdf on March 14, 2019.

Howard, E. R., Lindholm-Leary, K. J., Rogers, D., Olague, N., Medina, J., Kennedy, B., et al. (2018). *Guiding principles for dual language education* (3rd ed.). Washington, DC: Center for Applied Linguistics. Accessed at www.cal.org/resource-center/publications-products/guiding-principles-3rd-edition-pdf-download on March 14, 2019.

Howard, E. R., & Sugarman, J. (2011). *Realizing the vision of two-way immersion: Fostering effective programs and classrooms.* Washington, DC: Center for Applied Linguistics.

Howard, T. C. (2010). *Why race and culture matter in schools: Closing the achievement gap in America's classrooms.* New York: Teachers College Press.

Illinois State Board of Education. (2014). *Guidance on building teacher evaluation systems for teachers of students with disabilities, English learners, and early childhood students.* Accessed at www.isbe.net/documents/14-3-teacher-eval-sped-ell-preschool.pdf on March 14, 2019.

Jones, N. D., Buzick, H. M., & Turkan, S. (2013). Including students with disabilities and English learners in measures of educator effectiveness. *Educational Researcher, 42*(4), 234–241.

Kane, T. J., & Staiger, D. O. (2012). *Gathering feedback for teaching: Combining high-quality observations with student surveys and achievement gains.* Seattle, WA: Bill and Melinda Gates Foundation.

Kaye, B., & Jordan-Evans, S. (2003). *Love it, don't leave it: 26 ways to get what you want at work.* San Francisco: Berrett-Koehler.

Klump, J., & McNeir, G. (2005). *Culturally responsive practices for student success: A regional sampler.* Portland, OR: Northwest Regional Educational Laboratory. Accessed at https://educationnorthwest.org/sites/default/files/culturally-responsive-practices.pdf on March 14, 2019.

Knight, J. (2007). *Instructional coaching: A partnership approach to improving instruction.* Thousand Oaks, CA: Corwin Press.

Knight, J. (2009). *Instructional coaching: A multimedia kit for professional development.* Thousand Oaks, CA: Corwin Press.

Knight, J. (2014). *Focus on teaching: Using video for high-impact instruction.* Thousand Oaks, CA: Corwin Press.

Koole, T. (2012). Teacher evaluations: Assessing "knowing," "understanding," and "doing." In G. Rasmussen, C. E. Brouwer, & D. Day (Eds.), *Evaluating cognitive completeness in interaction* (pp. 43–66). Amsterdam, the Netherlands: Benjamins.

Koole, T. (2015). Classroom interaction. In K. Tracy (Ed.), *International encyclopedia of language and social interaction.* Hoboken, NJ: Wiley-Blackwell.

Kotter, J. P. (1996). *Leading change.* Boston: Harvard Business School Press.

Kotter, J. P. (2012). *Leading change.* Boston: Harvard Business Review Press.

Krashen, S. D. (1982). *Principles and practice in second language acquisition.* Oxford, England: Pergamon.

Krashen, S. D. (1987). *Principles and practices in second language acquisition.* Englewood Cliffs, NJ: Prentice Hall International.

Krashen, S., & Biber, D. (1988). *On course: Bilingual education's success in California.* Sacramento: California Association for Bilingual Education.

Kuhl, P. K. (2004). Early language acquisition: Cracking the speech code. *Nature Reviews Neuroscience, 5*(11), 831–843.

Kuhl, P. K. (2010). Brain mechanisms in early language acquisition. *Neuron, 67*(5), 713–727.

Ladson-Billings, G. (2001). *Crossing over to Canaan: The journey of new teachers in diverse classrooms.* San Francisco: Jossey-Bass.

Learning Sciences Marzano Center. (2017). *Success map, scales and evidences for the Marzano Focused Teacher Evaluation Model.* West Palm Beach, FL: Learning Sciences International. Accessed at www.kibsd.org/cms/lib/AK01801504/Centricity/Domain/4/KIBSD%20Appendix%20A%20Focused%20Teacher%20Eval%20Protocol%20w%20Map%2020170424.pdf on March 14, 2019.

Levine, D. U., & Lezotte, L. W. (1990). *Unusually effective schools: A review and analysis of research and practice.* Madison, WI: National Center for Effective Schools Research and Development.

Liebtag, E., & Haugen, C. (2015, May 14). *Shortage of dual-language teachers: Filling the gap* [Blog post]. Accessed at http://blogs.edweek.org/edweek/global_learning/2015/05/shortage_of_dual_language_teachers_filling_the_gap.html on March 14, 2019.

Lindholm-Leary, K. J. (2001). *Dual language education*. Clevedon, England: Dual-Language and Bilingual Matters.

Lindholm-Leary, K. J. (2005). The rich promise of two-way immersion. *Educational Leadership, 62*(4), 56–59.

Lindsey, R. B., Robins, K. N., & Terrell, R. D. (2009). *Cultural proficiency: A manual for school leaders*. Thousand Oaks, CA: Corwin Press.

Linville, H. A. (2016). ESOL teachers as advocates: An important role? *TESOL Journal, 7*(1), 98–131.

López, F. (2014, January). *Enhancing classroom observations with knowledge about effective teaching practices for ELLs*. Presented at the Using Observational and Student Achievement Data to Improve Teaching conference, University of Arizona, Tucson.

López, F., Scanlan, M., & Gundrum, B. (2013). Preparing teachers of English language learners: Empirical evidence and policy implications. *Education Policy Analysis Archives, 21*(20). Accessed at http://epaa.asu.edu/ojs/article/view/1132 on March 14, 2019.

Marshall, K. (2013). *Rethinking teacher supervision and evaluation: How to work smart, build collaboration, and close the achievement gap* (2nd ed.). San Francisco: Jossey-Bass.

Marzano, R. J. (n.d.). *Four Marzano teacher evaluation domains*. Accessed at www.marzanoevaluation.com/evaluation/four_domains_2014_Protocol on March 14, 2019.

Marzano, R. J. (2001a). *A new era of school reform: Going where the research takes us*. Aurora, CO: Mid-Continent Research for Education and Learning.

Marzano, R. J. (2001b). *Classroom instruction that works: Research-based strategies for increasing student achievement*. Alexandria, VA: Association for Supervision and Curriculum Development.

Marzano, R. J. (2003). *What works in schools: Translating research into action*. Alexandria, VA: Association for Supervision and Curriculum Development.

Marzano, R. J., & Toth, M. D. (2013). *Teacher evaluation that makes a difference: A new model for teacher growth and student achievement*. Alexandria, VA: Association for Supervision and Curriculum Development.

Massachusetts Department of Elementary and Secondary Education. (2009). *Presenting the growth model to a constituent group? Use the growth model PowerPoint*. Accessed at www.doe.mass.edu/mcas/growth on March 14, 2019.

Maxwell, L. A. (2014, August 19). U.S. school enrollment hits majority-minority milestone. *Education Week*. Accessed at www.edweek.org/ew/articles/2014/08/20/01demographics.h34.html on September 19, 2018.

McCaffrey, D. F., Hamilton, L. S., Stecher, B. M., Klein, S. P., Bugliari, D., & Robyn, A. (2001). Interactions among instructional practices, curriculum, and student achievement: The case of standards-based high school mathematics. *Journal for Research in Mathematics Education, 32*(5), 493–517.

McManus, S. (2008). *Attributes of effective formative assessment.* Paper prepared for the Formative Assessment of Teachers and Students, State Collaborative on Assessment and Student Standards of the Council of Chief State School Officers, Washington, DC.

Mercer, N. (2004). Sociocultural discourse analysis: Analysing classroom talk as a social mode of thinking. *Journal of Applied Linguistics, 1*(2), 137–168.

Mitchell, C. (2019, March 19). Bilingual teachers are in short supply: How can schools cultivate their own? *Education Week.* Accessed at http://blogs.edweek.org/edweek /learning-the language/2019/03/bilingual_teachers_shortage.html on March 14, 2019.

Moll, L. C., Amanti, C., Neff, D., & Gonzalez, N. (1992). Funds of knowledge for teaching: Using a qualitative approach to connect homes and classrooms. *Theory Into Practice, 31*(2), 132–141.

National Comprehensive Center for Teacher Quality. (2012, July). *Summary of "expert forum on the evaluation of teachers of English language learners."* Accessed at www .gtlcenter.org/sites/default/files/docs/ForumSummary_July2012.pdf on March 14, 2019.

National Education Association. (2015). *How educators can advocate for English language learners: All in!* Accessed at www.colorincolorado.org/sites/default/files /ELL_AdvocacyGuide2015.pdf on March 18, 2019.

National Institute for Excellence in Teaching. (2012). *Career teacher handbook: TAP instructional rubrics.* Accessed at www.mccormick.k12.sc.us/cms/lib/SC01001536 /Centricity/Domain/388/Career%20Teacher%20Handbook-TAP%20 Instructional%20Rubrics.pdf on March 14, 2019.

New York Department of Education. (n.d.a). *Language Allocation Policy (LAP).* New York: Author. Accessed at www.cfn107.org/uploads/6/1/9/2/6192492/lap_guidance .pdf on September 4, 2019.

New York Department of Education. (n.d.b). *Specific considerations for teachers of English language learners.* Accessed at https://weteachnyc.org/resources/resource /specific-considerations-teachers-english-language-learners on March 14, 2019.

Otheguy, R., García, O., & Reid, W. (2015). Clarifying translanguaging and deconstructing named languages: A perspective from linguistics. *Applied Linguistics Review, 6*(3), 281–307.

Paradis, J., Genesee, F., & Crago, M. B. (2004). *Dual language development and disorders: A handbook on bilingualism and second language learning.* Baltimore: Brookes.

Paradis, J., Genesee, F., & Crago, M. B. (2011). *Dual language development and disorders: A handbook on bilingualism and second language learning* (2nd ed.). Baltimore: Brookes.

Park, M., O'Toole, A., & Katsiaficas, C. (2017, October). *Dual language learners: A demographic and policy profile for California*. Washington, DC: Migration Policy Institute.

Park, M., Zong, J., & Batalova, J. (2018). *Growing superdiversity among young U.S. dual language learners and its implications*. Washington, DC: Migration Policy Institute.

Pawan, F., & Craig, D. (2011). ESL and content area teacher responses to discussions on English language learner instruction. *TESOL Journal, 2*(3), 293–311.

Pennsylvania Department of Education. (2013). *Possible guiding questions: Conversations between principals and teachers—ROLE: English as a second language teachers*. Accessed at http://dev.static.pdesas.org/content/documents/Guiding%20Questions%20for%20English%20as%20a%20Second%20Language%20Teachers.pdf on March 14, 2019.

Pianta, R. C., & Hamre, B. K. (2009). Conceptualization, measurement, and improvement of classroom processes: Standardized observation can leverage capacity. *Educational Researcher, 38*(2), 109–119.

Pianta, R. C., La Paro, K. M., & Hamre, B. K. (2008). *Classroom assessment scoring system (CLASS) manual, pre-K*. Baltimore: Brookes.

Pinker, S. (1994). *The language instinct: How the mind creates language*. New York: HarperCollins.

Podhajski, B., Mather, N., Nathan, J., & Sammons, J. (2009). Professional development in scientifically based reading instruction: Teacher knowledge and reading outcomes. *Journal of Learning Disabilities, 42*(5), 403–417.

Popham, W. J. (2010). *Everything school leaders need to know about assessment*. Thousand Oaks, CA: Corwin Press.

Popkewitz, T. S. (1991, September). *A political/sociological critique of teacher education reforms: Evaluation of the relation of power and knowledge*. Presented at the Second National Research Symposium on Limited English Proficient Student Issues, Washington, DC.

Reeves, D. B., & DuFour, R. B. (2018, February). Next generation accountability: How district leadership can best respond to the Every Student Succeeds Act to establish meaningful evaluation. *AASA School Administrator*. Accessed at http://my.aasa.org/AASA/Resources/SAMag/2018/Feb18/ReevesDuFour.aspx on March 14, 2019.

Rivera, M. O., Francis, D. J., Fernandez, M., Moughamian, A. C., Jergensen, J., & Lesaux, N. K. (2010). *Effective practices for English language learners: Principals from five states speak*. Portsmouth, NH: RMC Research Corporation.

Rosen, R., & Parise, L. M. (2017, March). *Using evaluation systems for teacher improvement: Are school districts ready to meet new federal goals?* Accessed at https://files.eric.ed.gov/fulltext/ED574046.pdf on March 14, 2019.

Safty, A. (1992). French immersion: Bilingual education and unilingual administration. *Interchange, 23*(4), 389–405.

Samson, J. F., & Collins, B. A. (2012, April). *Preparing all teachers to meet the needs of English language learners: Applying research to policy and practice for teacher effectiveness.* Accessed at https://files.eric.ed.gov/fulltext/ED535608.pdf on March 13, 2019.

Scheerens, J., & Bosker, R. J. (1997). *The foundations of educational effectiveness.* Oxford, England: Pergamon.

Scholes, P. A. (2010). *The development of two units for basic training and resources for teaching English to speakers of other languages: "Basic principles of second language acquisition" and "Communicative language teacher and information gap exercises"* (Master's selected project). Provo, UT: Brigham Young University.

Shavelson, R. J. (2006). On the integration of formative assessment in teaching and learning: Implications for new pathways in teacher education. In F. Oser, F. Achtenhagen, & U. Renold (Eds.), *Competence-oriented teacher training: Old research demands and new pathways* (pp. 63–78). Utrecht, the Netherlands: Sense Publishers.

Shavelson, R. J., Yin, Y., Furtak, E. M., Ruiz-Primo, M. A., Ayala, C. C., Young, D. B., et al. (2008). On the role and impact of formative assessment on science inquiry teaching and learning. In J. E. Coffey, R. Douglas, & C. Stearns (Eds.), *Assessing science learning: Perspectives from research and practice* (pp. 21–36). Washington, DC: NSTA Press.

Short, D. J., & Fitzsimmons, S. (2007). *Double the work: Challenges and solutions to acquiring language and academic literacy for adolescent English language learners—A report to Carnegie Corporation of New York.* Washington, DC: Alliance for Excellent Education.

Slavin, R. E., Lake, C., Chambers, B., Cheung, A., & Davis, S. (2009). Effective reading programs for the elementary grades: A best-evidence synthesis. *Review of Educational Research, 79*(4), 1391–1466.

Soltero, S. W. (2016). *Dual language education: Program design and implementation.* Portsmouth, NH: Heinemann.

Spolsky, B. (1989). *Conditions for second language learning.* Oxford, England: Oxford University Press.

Strong, W. (1986). *Creative approaches to sentence combining.* Washington, DC: Office of Educational Research and Improvement.

Thomas, W. P., & Collier, V. P. (2002). *A national study of school effectiveness for language minority students' long-term academic achievement.* Santa Cruz, CA: Center for Research on Education, Diversity and Excellence.

Thomas, W. P., & Collier, V. P. (2012). *Dual language education for a transformed world.* Albuquerque, NM: Fuentes Press.

Tivnan, T., & Hemphill, L. (2005). Comparing four literacy reform models in high-poverty schools: Patterns of first-grade achievement. *Elementary School Journal, 105*(5), 419–441.

U.S. Department of Education, Office of English Language Acquisition. (2015). *Dual language education programs: Current state policies and practices.* Washington, DC: American Institutes for Research.

Villegas, A. M., & Lucas, T. (2002). Preparing culturally responsive teachers: Rethinking the curriculum. *Journal of Teacher Education, 53*(1), 20–32.

Vogt, M. E., Echevarría, J., & Washam, M. A. (2015). *99 more ideas and activities for teaching English learners with the SIOP model.* Boston: Pearson.

Vygotsky, L. S. (1962). *Thought and language.* Cambridge, MA: MIT Press.

Warger, C. (2001). *Cultural reciprocity aids collaboration with families.* Arlington, VA: ERIC Clearinghouse on Disabilities and Gifted Education.

White, M. E. (2002). *Evaluating the bilingual teacher: A monolingual administrator's challenge.* Presented at the annual meeting of the National Association of African American Studies, the National Association of Hispanic and Latino Studies, the National Association of Native American Studies, and the National Association of Asian Studies, Houston, TX.

WIDA Consortium. (2010). *The cornerstone of the WIDA standards: Guiding principles of language development.* Madison: Board of Regents of the University of Wisconsin System, University of Wisconsin-Madison. Accessed at https://wida.wisc.edu/sites /default/files/resource/Guiding-Principles-of-Language-Development.pdf on March 14, 2019.

WIDA Consortium. (2013). *Developing a culturally and linguistically responsive approach to response to instruction and intervention (RtI²) for English language learners.* Madison: Board of Regents of the University of Wisconsin System, University of Wisconsin-Madison. Accessed at https://uab.edu/education/esl/images /WIDA_RtI2_forELLs.pdf on August 15, 2019.

Wiggins, G., & McTighe, J. (2005). *Understanding by design* (2nd ed.). Alexandria, VA: Association for Supervision and Curriculum Development.

Williams, C. P. (2015, April 9). *Interview: Improving training for teachers of dual language learners* [Blog post]. Accessed at https://newamerica.org/education-policy /edcentral/spreadthewordsbouteillon on March 14, 2019.

Zwiers, J., O'Hara, S., & Pritchard, R. (2014). *Common Core standards in diverse classrooms: Essential practices for developing academic language and disciplinary literacy.* Portland, ME: Stenhouse.

Index

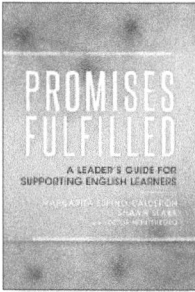

Promises Fulfilled
Margarita Espino Calderón and Shawn Slakk With Hector Montenegro
Discover research-based strategies preK–12 administrators and teacher leaders can implement to effectively identify and support English learners. Each chapter ends with discussion questions readers should share with staff or team members to promote EL success schoolwide.
BKF774

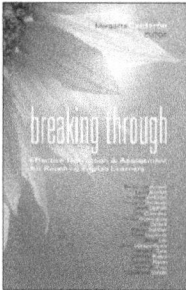

Breaking Through
Edited by Margarita Espino Calderón
Utilizing research and field studies, this book outlines a whole-school approach to helping English learners achieve. Discover how integrating language, literacy, and subject matter instruction leads to greater success for this growing student population.
BKF552

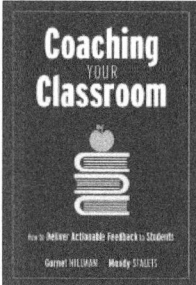

Coaching Your Classroom
Garnet Hillman and Mandy Stalets
In *Coaching Your Classroom*, the authors share a fresh perspective on classroom feedback for all grade levels and content areas. Explore the parallels between classroom teaching and athletic coaching, and learn how to employ specific coaching techniques to create a student-centered culture in your classroom.
BKF845

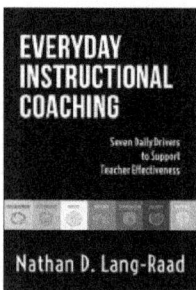

Everyday Instructional Coaching
Nathan D. Lang
Discover seven drivers you can use to improve your daily coaching practices: collaboration, transparency, inquiry, discourse, reverberation, sincerity, and influence. Each of the book's chapters defines, describes, and offers tips for implementing one of the seven drivers.
BKF802